DRAKE

An unofficial compilation of fun, facts and trivia about your favourite celebrity, listed from A to Zee.

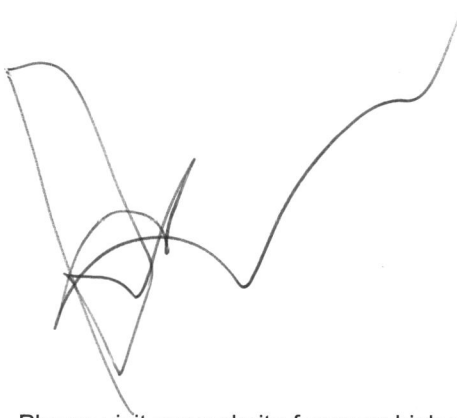

Please visit our website for more high-quality books

www.celebrityatozee.com

Celebrity A to Zee

Front/Back Cover illustration: cm2creative

Printed by: Asia Korea Printing Inc

CONTENTS

A

B

C

Aaliyah

On 25 August 2010, nine years after Aaliyah's tragic death, Drake wrote an open letter – released onto the internet – to her, expressing his admiration for her work and her passion for music. He also paid homage to the 'Princess of R&B' by sampling her song; At Your Best on the single Unforgettable, from his debut studio album, Thank Me Later.

Born in Brooklyn, New York City on 16 January 1979, Aaliyah Dana Haughton was raised in Detroit and attended the Detroit High School for the Performing Arts. Always wanting to entertain, she performed in various school plays, TV shows and commercials. At the age of ten she appeared on the television show *Star Search* and frequently performed in concert alongside Gladys Knight, who was married to her Uncle Barry Hankerson. Aaliyah signed with Jive Records in 1991 and released her debut album, Age Ain't Nothing But A Number, aged 14 in 1994. The album was produced and partly written by American R&B star R Kelly and was well received by the critics, peaking at number eighteen on the Billboard 200. The album – which included two hit singles, Back and Forth and At Your Best (You Are Love) – was certified triple platinum by the Recording Industry Association of America (RIAA) (see **Recording Industry Association of America**) with sales of over 3 million copies.

After ending her contract with Jive Records in 1996, Aaliyah signed with Atlantic Records and released her second album, One In A Million, produced by Timbaland and Missy Elliot later that year.

The album went on to sell over 3.7 million copies in the United States and over 8 million copies worldwide. The lead single from the album, If Your Girl Only Knew, topped the Billboard Hot R&B/Hip-Hop Song list for two weeks.

In 2000, Aaliyah appeared in her first major film, *Romeo Must Die,* also contributing to the film's soundtrack with the single from the film, Try Again, earning her a Grammy Award Nomination for Best Female R&B Vocal Performance. On 25 August 2001, Aaliyah and eight others were killed in an aeroplane crash in the Bahamas, shortly after filming the music video for the single, Rock the Boat on the island. She was just 22 years old.

Acknowledging her as an early influence on him and his music, Drake sometimes wears a picture of Aaliyah on his ear piece while performing (see **Photographs**) and finishes some of his shows with an Aaliyah tribute, or name check. In his letter, Drake relives the moment he heard the tragic news of her death and tells the 'Princess of R&B' that he was one of her biggest fans, thanks her for her inspiration and regrets never having had the chance to meet or hang out with her.

Drake has a number of tattoos paying homage to the Try Again star, with her face tattooed onto the right-hand side of his back, and the numbers 416 inked onto his right side. The numbers represent the telephone area code for his home city of Toronto, however the number 4 in the sequence is only partially coloured so that it appears like the number 1 and the three digits together appear as 116 – Aaliyah's birthday is 16 January or 1/16. (see **Tattoos**)

Aaliyah: Enough Said

On 5 August 2012, Drake released a posthumous duet with Aaliyah, on a previously unheard vocal she had laid down prior to her untimely death, called Enough Said.

Drizzy had previously hinted that he was planning a posthumous collaboration with the star and the song was released on the Blackground Records label, but it failed to make any significant impact in the charts. The track, which was produced by Noah '40' Shebib, features Aaliyah's unreleased vocal with Drake adding his own verses.

Drake has stated that he also has ambitions to release an album of 14 songs with the blessing of Aaliyah's family, label, and management. The album will feature as yet unreleased vocals from Aaliyah and the intention is to involve people who have contributed to her past success, but no release date has yet been confirmed.

Abrams Norbert

Norbert Abrams is one of the Noble Caplan Abrams talent agency's well known agents. Originally called Noble Talent Management, the agency is one of the biggest in Canada, and famed for developing young stars into the brilliant actors of tomorrow. Based in Toronto, Ontario, the agency has represented many of Canada's most prestigious high-profile stars for over 25 years and is well-known for representing its clients in a friendly and professional manner, with its stable of performers involved in film, television, theatre, animation, and musical theatre.

Norbert Abrams, with a background in International Advertising and Marketing, has held many posts during a varied career including the Head of the Young Talent Division and has vast experience in the entertainment industry. Abrams has always endeavored to develop and promote the careers of his clients and he represented Aubrey Graham during the time that he was appearing in *Degrassi: The Next Generation*. Fan mail sent to Graham during this time was directed to the company address at 1260 Yonge Street, Toronto.

Acting

Drake has been involved with acting and the stage since his mother signed him onto the books of a Toronto talent agency at the tender age of five. During this period he appeared in numerous commercials, magazines and advertisements for major companies such as Sears, GMC and Toys R Us. He was also a member of the Young People's Theatre based at 165 Front Street East, Toronto, Ontario (see **Young People's Theatre**). Every Saturday morning, Aubrey's father Dennis dropped him off at the theatre and he remembers thinking to himself after one such journey 'there's no way them kids are gonna' do anything positive or make a living from the stage, because they were always so unruly.'

While he attended the Forest Hill Collegiate Institute (see **Forest Hill Collegiate Institute**), Aubrey was signed up to an acting agency by the father of one of his classmates, who was looking for a young actor. He asked his son if he had any friends who made his classmates laugh and he mentioned a certain Aubrey Graham to his father. After a brief introduction Aubrey was immediately signed up to the agency.

Drake remembers:

> 'I was in class, and I used to always crack jokes. I was a good liar and a good talker. And this kid in my class was like, 'Yo my dad is an agent. You should go talk to him because you're good and you make people laugh.' I was just good, I was my father's son, I was slick, you know? When it comes to knowing what to say, to charm, I always had it.'

In 2000, Graham attended numerous auditions for a new Canadian TV teen drama about life at a Toronto high school called *Degrassi: The Next Generation,* little knowing that it would change his life forever.

The auditions were scheduled over a number of months, until one day his mother called him to return home from school, which was conveniently situated just across the road from where they were living at the time, to receive the call from the show's executives to inform him that he had won the part of basketball player Jimmy Brooks. He remembers jumping up and down shouting 'I got it! I got it!'

In 2001, he also succeeded in winning the part as Joey Tamarin in *Blue Murder* – a Canadian crime drama television series – featuring in an episode called Remembrance Day: Part 1, which aired on 26 March.

Degrassi: The Next Generation series premiered on 14 October 2001, and Aubrey Graham's first appearance as Jimmy Brooks occurred in Season 1: Episode 3 called *Family Politics*, which aired on 4 November, when he was just 15 years old. During the show he had to draw on all his acting skills and emotions, covering the usual angst of a teenager growing up. This was especially so during Season 4 of the series, when his character Jimmy Brooks became disabled from the waist down after being shot by his classmate Rick Murray. In the story Murray was angry with Brooks, who he had wrongly accused of humiliating him during a school quiz competition.

Drake later remembered that he was quite apprehensive about having to play a disabled character after the shooting, due to him not having any experience of disability, or how people might react to him personally. After talking the role through with his mother and the series writers, he decided that the role would be a perfect opportunity to highlight the difficulties that wheelchair users face in carrying out their daily activities and would also give him the chance to publicise his acting skills to a wider audience, as the show was becoming more popular in the US.

Io add realism to the character he decided to join a wheelchair user for the day in order to help him gain an insight into the difficulties they frequently encounter while shopping in malls, travelling on public transport and the general reaction of the public to the disabled. After being inspired by his disabled mentor he decided not to play the role as a victim, but to accept the cards that he had been dealt with and to play the Jimmy Brooks character in a positive manner, with him really embracing the role of a disabled teenager. He eventually mastered the titanium wheelchair so well that he used to career down the corridors of the school where filming for *Degrassi* took place, becoming so adept that the crew nicknamed him 'Mr Mobility'.

In 2008, the producers of *Degrassi: The Next Generation* decided to move the show in a different direction, which included the removal of numerous familiar characters from the series, including that of Graham's character Jimmy Brooks. His role on the show finally ended in 2009, when the Jimmy Brooks character graduated from Degrassi High and moved to New York. Graham eventually appeared in a total of 138 episodes of the series.

Along with the other members of the cast, Graham won the Young Artist Award for the Best Ensemble in a TV Series (Comedy or Drama) in 2002-2003 for *Degrassi: The Next Generation* (see **Young Artist Award**).

Drake as the hip-hop/rap artist is mentioned in the 2010 television film *Degrassi: Takes Manhattan*, making him one of only two actors from the show – along with Shenae Grimes – that exist within the series fictional universe, independently of their characters on the show.

Aubrey Graham continued to pursue his acting career for a short time after leaving the show, with further roles in TV series including, *Sophie and Beyond the Break*, but he found the process of auditions, screen tests and the waiting around between takes particularly frustrating, with scenes sometimes taking up to a couple of days to film, or future projects having to wait months to get the green light to finally commence filming due to financial constraints. So when he was finally written out of the show in 2008, he decided to devote all his energy to his real passion, music.

Talking about his time on *Degrassi: The Next Generation*, Drake has said that a normal day's filming would begin with his rising at 5am for a 6am start on set, and then finish sometime between 6pm to 7pm with an hour's lunch break. During downtime between his scenes he developed a passion for playing pool, often beating the other cast members in games for money especially his close friend Shane Kippel – Spinner in the show – who ended up losing numerous games and money to the pool shark Graham.

In May 2013 Drake returned to acting with a cameo role – along with Kanye West – in the film *Anchorman 2: The Legend Continues* and was pictured filming his scenes in New York wearing an afro wig. (see **Photographs**) The film is set for UK release in December 2013.

Acting Career History

Title	Year	Character	No
Drake's Film appearances:			
Jew Jube Lives	2004	Doo-rag guy	
Jay and Silent Bob do Degrassi	2005	Jimmy Brooks	
Degrassi: Spring Break Movie	2008	Jimmy Brooks	
Charlie Bartlett	2008	A/V Jones	
Mookie's Law	2008	Chet Walters	
Breakaway	2011	Cameo	
Ice Age 4: The Continental Drift	2012	Ethan	
Anchorman 2:The Legend Continues	2013	Cameo	
Drake's TV appearances:			
Blue Murder	2001	Joey Tamarin	1
Degrassi: The Next Generation	2001 - 09	Jimmy Brooks	138
Soul Food	2002	Fredrick	1
Conviction	2002	Teen Fish	1
Best Friend's Date	2002	Dater	1
Radio Free Roscoe	2004	Caller	1
Instant Star	2005	Himself	1
The Border	2008	PFC Harvey	1
Being Erica	2008	Ken	1
Sophie	2009	Ken	1
Beyond The Break	2009	Himself	1
Punk'd	2012	Himself	1

Afro

As a teenager in Toronto, Drake had what his friends used to call a 'terrible fro' and they often recall how embarrassed they were when they hung around with him. Eventually, his good friend Niko (see **Carino 'Niko' Nicholas**) introduced him to Jason Macaraig, a barber who worked at the Forum Barber Parlor in Toronto and encouraged him to have his Afro cut. On the day of the haircut, J-Mac remembers he saw this guy come into his shop with what he said was a really bad head and after a heated discussion, Drake was eventually persuaded into changing his style. After J-Mac had done his 'fade' Drake has said that since that day, his new look has helped him feel more confident and a whole new person was born.

Drake remembers:

'When I was 17, I used to have this terrible Afro, you know, an Afro is supposed to be big, it's supposed to be a nice sphere and then it's supposed to end. My joint never really ended, it was like a neck Afro and it made me look like I had the biggest head in the world. It got so bad that Niko demanded I find a new barber. After following that advice he got a new hairdo and his life has never been the same. 'I was a whole new person, I was, like, reborn' he laughed.

Drake's cut consisted of: ¼ Inch Wave Cut, Mid Bald Fade with a Sharp Hairline.

J-Mac gets a name check in Drake's song, Good Life from the I Am Toronto mixtape, and continues to cut for the OVO crew as well as stars Nas, Mack Maine, French Montana and Trey Songz. (see **J-Mac**)

Albums (Studio) Released

Drake's first studio album, Thank Me Later was released on 15 June 2010, on the Young Money Entertainment, Cash Money Record labels and distributed by Universal Motown Records. The album – originally planned to be called The Search – debuted at number one on the US Billboard 200 chart, with first week sales of over 447,000 copies. It has since been certified platinum by the Recording Industry Association of America, having sold over 1,700,000 copies in the US since its 2010 release.

Recorded in various studios in the US and Canada during 2009-10, Drake announced he had submitted the final copy of the album to the assembled crowd at the University of Missouri during his Away From Home tour on 26 April. The album has gone on to produce four singles: Over, the lead single which Drake premiered on Toronto's radio station *Flow 93.5*, Find Your Love and Billboard hits, Fancy and Miss Me featuring Lil Wayne.

Drake said:

> 'I went with Over as the first single because of the words in the hook being the most repetitive part. I have a lot of great songs on the album, but the biggest thing was the opening line on the hook.'

The album, at just over one hour in length, delves into Drake's inner feelings of doubt, insecurity and heartbreak and was received favourably by both fans and critics alike. The majority of the tracks on the album were produced by Noah '40' Shebib and Matthew 'Boi-1da' Samuels, who had also produced the hit singles, Best I Ever Had and Forever.

Drake's second studio album, Take Care, was released through Young Money Entertainment and Cash Money Record Labels on 15 November 2011. The album was released in three versions: the standard edition, the birthday edition and the OG Ron C chopped and screwed edition.

On 8 October 2011, Drake announced on his OVO blog that Take Care would be released on 15 November, later than the original scheduled release date of 24 October – Drake's birthday – due to the difficulty of getting three samples cleared on time. The title for the album was partly due to his previous album in his words 'being rushed'. He was determined to take his time and get everything right. The name apparently came to Drake while he was travelling on the tour bus en route to the stadium in Birmingham, England for a gig. He said of his previous album:

> 'I didn't get to take the time that I had wanted on that record, I rushed a lot of the songs and sonically I didn't get to sit with the record and say 'I should change this verse'. Once it was done, it was done. That's why my new album is called Take Care, because I get to take my time this go-round.'

On its eventual release, the album shot straight to number one on the US Billboard 200 chart, with over 631,000 sales in the first week, eventually staying on the chart for 33 weeks. The album went on to top the Billboard Rap Albums and R&B/Hip-Hop Albums in its debut week and was certified platinum by the Recording Industry Association of America, selling over 1,810,000 copies.

In the United Kingdom, Take Care entered the charts at number five, with sales of over 100,000 and was certified gold on 16 December 2011, by the British Recorded Music Industry (BPI).

Drake's third studio album, Nothing Was the Same was released on 24 September 2013 onto Drake's OVO Sound, Young Money, Cash Money and Republic labels. The album contained 13 tracks, with 2 bonus tracks available on the deluxe version and was recorded in Los Angeles and the Metalworks Studio in Toronto. The lead single from the album, Started From the Bottom – produced by Mike Zombie and '40' – was released on 6 February and certified double platinum by the RIAA for selling over 1,700,000 copies in August 2013.

On 24 September, the day the album hit the shelves and iTunes, Drake made an in-store appearance at NYC Best Buy at 622 Broadway.

All Things Fresh

All Things Fresh (ATF) is the name Drake and his crew called themselves in the early days around Toronto. They started out as a group of friends hanging out in and around Toronto looking for a good time and he reps the crew on the song Thank Me Now from his debut album, Thank Me Later. The crew would have dinner and drink champagne in the bars and clubs, with the aim that people would take notice of them. It was also around this time that Drake was driving around the City in a leased Rolls Royce. All Things Fresh was originally – and mostly still is – a group of Drake's closest friends consisting of Boi-1da, 40, Niko, D10, Oliver, Karla, Hush, T-RexXx, Chubbs, CJ, P Reign, Courtne and Andreena Mill. Drake has rapped 'All Things Fresh' in many of his songs with his early mixtapes also released on the ATF label. The logo ATF also features on Drake's early clothing lines.

Allthings-fresh.net

The official Drake fan site – Allthings-fresh.net – was founded in 2007 by Karla 'hustlegrl' Moy as a means for fans to keep in touch with all things Drake.

Formed before his meteoric rise to international stardom, the site had supported the young rapper through hosting content related to his career, information on upcoming gigs, his MySpace page and exclusive material for fans to access.

After years of success, the site was closed on 28 November 2011, with Moy posting the following announcement, along with a thank you to all of the site's visitors for supporting her efforts throughout the years.

> 'Thank you for visiting the All Things Fresh site during these past few years and throughout the musical journey, for which, you will forever be in our debt. You're all really appreciated. I'm on the verge of starting a new chapter in my life so it was simply time for me to move on and explore other opportunities. ATF is still a part of me and I am so thankful for being a part of it.'

Moy has gone on to work with numerous acts signed to Universal Records and helped launch Lil Wayne, Bryant Management and Funkmaster Flex's websites, with Karen Civil. She is currently working on two new projects, Ro Ransom and JMSN.

Alleyne Hyghly/Taylor Lamar

Hyghly Alleyne and Lamar Taylor of the XO crew have both been a part of Drake's rise to fame since they were introduced in 2010.

Alleyne, along with his partner Lamar Taylor photographed the covers for Drake's Thank Me Later and Take Care albums. They are also credited with directing the music videos for some of Drake's most popular songs such as Marvin's Room and Headlines, which was filmed in Toronto and showcased some of the city's major landmarks.

The final scene of the Headlines video shows Drake standing centre field at the Rogers Centre, with the retractable roof closing above him and the motto 'Take Care' emblazoned onto the electronic scoreboard.

In 2011, the duo directed the video for the gold certified single Marvin's Room, as well as providing Drake's official photography for the shoot. The same year they directed the music video for The Motto, the triple platinum single taken off Drake's second studio album, Take Care. Due to the success of the song it was awarded the Hip-Hop Video of the Year at the MuchMusic Video Awards, with Alleyne accepting the award on behalf of himself, Lamar Taylor and Drake on Sunday 17 June 2012 at the MuchMusic headquarters in Toronto. They continue to work with Drake.

Interestingly in 2009 after studying Art at university, the duo formed the company; She's So Lovely with Abel Tesfaye, aka The Weeknd, with the aim to create the link between video, photography and music. They also designed the artwork for most of The Weeknd's early mixtapes. (see **The Weeknd**)

Alleyne & Taylor's Music Videos featuring Drake

Year	Artist	Single	Album
2011	Drake	Headlines	Take Care
2011	Drake	Marvin's Room	Take Care
2011	Drake	The Motto	Take Care

American Idol

American Idol is a reality singing talent contest, which premiered on Fox TV in 2002 and is one of the most successful in the history of American TV.

14

The show has a judging panel made up of well known celebrities with different experiences of the music industry, who critique the performance of each contestant. In Season 12, the panel consisted of Drake's fellow Young Money member Nicki Minaj, who may have had something to do with his surprise appearance on the show.

Drake made an appearance on the show on 25 April 2013, to surprise one of the final contestants Candice Glover, who had performed his song, Find Your Love the previous evening. As Drake spoke about how much he liked her interpretation of his song and would welcome performing a duet with her, Candice thought she was listening to an audio message from the rapper. Drake ignited a wave of applause as he walked onto the stage, leaving Candice understandably speechless. Drake went on to hint at a possible collaboration on a track with her before the show went to a commercial break. Candice eventually went on to be crowned the winner of the show.

The first winner of the contest, Kelly Clarkson, has gone on to win three Grammy Awards in her career and the show continues to produce talented artists who achieve commercial success.

American Music Awards

The American Music Awards is an annual awards ceremony, created in 1973 and is televised on ABC Television. Unlike the Grammy Awards, the American Music Awards are decided by public polls, record sales and other factors including video views and social networking activity. Some music industry experts believe that they more accurately reflect popular opinion than the Grammy Awards, which are decided by panels of Recording Academy members. Drake made his first performance at the awards when he performed his single Headlines backed by a live band on 20 November 2011 at the Nokia Theatre, Los Angeles. (see **Photographs**)

Nominated five times, Drake has failed to win an award to date.

Year	Nominated Work	Award	Result
2010	Drake	Rap/Hip-Hop Artist	Nominated
2010	Thank Me Later	Rap/Hip-Hop Album of the Year	Nominated
2012	Drake	Artist of the Year	Nominated
2012	Drake	Rap/Hip-Hop Artist	Nominated
2012	Take Care	Rap/Hip-Hop Album of the Year	Nominated

American Society of Composers, Authors and Publishers

The American Society of Composers, Authors and Publishers (ASCAP) is a not-for-profit performance rights organization which protects its members' musical copyright by monitoring public performances of their music, whether via broadcast or live performance and compensating them for their work. Drake has received five awards from the company to date.

Drake who had previously been with rival company, Broadcast Music Inc (BMI) finally joined ASCAP in April 2013 joining his producer Noah Shebib – who won the 2013 ASCAP Songwriter of the Year Award – and Boi-1da, who were already with the organisation.

ASCAP Awards won by Drake

Year	Nominated Work	Award	Result
2010	Best I Ever Had	Most Performed Song	Won
2010	Every Girl (with Young Money)	Most Performed Song	Won
2011	Forever	Most Performed Song	Won
2011	I'm On One (with DJ Khaled)	Most Performed Song	Won
2012	What's My Name? (with Rihanna)	Most Performed Song	Won

America's Most Wanted Tour

In the summer of 2009, while he was still a newcomer to the wider audiences, Drake joined three of hip-hop's biggest stars for a 21 city tour of the USA, as part of the Young Money Presents: America's Most Wanted Music Festival. The shows featured performances by Soulja Boy, Young Jeezy and Lil Wayne. The final part of the show included a musical tribute to the recently departed Michael Jackson featuring many of his hits. The tour kicked off on 27 July at the Toyota Pavilion Scranton, Pennsylvania with Drake being lowered via a platform onto the stage, owing to his recently torn anterior cruciate ligament injury to his right knee, which he sustained while playing basketball with friends. Due to be one of the headline acts, his planned 30-minute set was shortened to a special guest spot during Lil Wayne's set.

Drake began his set with Successful.

Young Money Presents: America's Most Wanted Tour Venues

July
07-27: Scranton, PA. Toyota Pavilion
07-29: Saratoga, NY. Performing Arts Center
07-30: Pittsburgh, PA. Post Gazette Pavilion
07-31: Philadelphia, PA. Susquehanna Bank Center

August
08-01: Wantagh, NY. Jones Beach Theater
08-02: Virginia Beach, VA. Verizon Wireless Amphitheater
08-04: Toronto, Ontario. Molson Amphitheater
08-05: Montreal, Quebec. Bell Centre
08-06: Cleveland, OH. Blossom Pavilion
08-07: Washington, DC. Nissan Pavilion
08-08: Raleigh, NC. Walnut Creek Amphitheater
08-09: Atlanta, GA. Lakewood Amphitheater
08-12: Phoenix, AZ. Cricket Wireless Amphitheater
08-13: Los Angeles, CA. Gibson Amphitheatre
08-14: Irvine, CA. Verizon Wireless Amphitheater
08-15: Concord, CA. Sleep Train Pavilion
08-17: Vancouver, British Columbia. GM Place
08-18: Edmonton, Alberta. Rexall Place
08-20: Denver, CO. Fiddler's Green Amphitheater
08-22: Houston, TX. Cynthia Woods Mitchell Pavilion
08-23: Dallas, TX. Superpages.com Center

Prior to the tour, Drake had been having acupuncture in an attempt to reduce the swelling on his knee, and had been advised to wear a brace while performing. His doctor had originally advised the rapper to take a couple of weeks off touring so that his injury would have sufficient time to heal properly. But Drake felt that he would be letting his fans and fellow Young Money artists down, so he decided to go ahead with the tour and to help build the newly emerging Young Money Entertainment brand.

Unfortunately during the third leg of the tour on Friday 31 July at the Susquehanna Bank Center, Camden New Jersey, Drake collapsed on stage while performing his hit single Best I Ever Had, further injuring his knee. Chris Brown replaced Drake in Brown's home state of Virginia on the Virginia Beach leg of the tour. Pleasure P, Jeremih and Young Money's Nicki Minaj joined the tour to replace Drake at various venues.

Drake ended up missing the next two shows, but then surprised everyone when he appeared with Trey Songz during Wayne's set on 4 August in Toronto to perform their hit single Successful. Performing while leaning on a stool, after his set he said to the crowd 'you know I would never let my city down' before limping off with the aid of a walking stick.

Due to the phenomenal demand from fans, eleven more shows were added to the tour, which finally ended at the Bank Atlantic Center in Sunrise, Florida on 6 September. The extra dates were as follows:

August
08-24 Kansas City, MO. Starlight Theatre
08-27 Darien Center, NY. Darien Lake Theme Park Resort
08-28 Noblesville, IN. Verizon Wireless Music Center
08-29 Tinley Park, IL. First Midwest Bank Amphitheater
08-30 Clarkston, MI.DTE Energy Music Theatre

September
09-01 St Paul, MN. Xcel Energy Center
09-02 Milwaukee, WI. Marcus Amphitheater
09-03 Cincinnati, OH. PNC Pavilion
09-04 Charlotte, NC. Verizon Wireless Amphitheatre
09-05 Tampa, FL. Ford Ampitheatre
09-06 Sunrise, FL. Bank Atlantic Center

Drake underwent surgery on his knee in Toronto on 8 September.

On 25 March 2013, Lil Wayne announced that the second America's Most Wanted Festival tour would be hitting 40 cities across the US, starting on 5 July 2013 and that it would last for 2 months with French Montana, Future and T.I. as support. The announcement of the tour corresponded with the release of Wayne's album, I Am Not A Human Being 2, in March 2013, which sold over 200,000 copies in the first week of its release. The album featured Drake on the platinum certified single, Love Me.

Area Code 416

Established in 1947, area code 416 is one of the original 86 telephone area codes of North America and is still used in central Toronto. The Toronto area code system has already undergone many changes since its creation, due to the expansion of the city and increased telephone usage. In the early years of the 20th century, the segments of the Toronto area code outside the city centre were separated to form area code 905. The split later produced some friendly rivalry between area code 416 owners and the owners of the new area code. Those residing within the city of Toronto are at times referred to as the 416ers, while those that live outside of the city are called the 905ers.

Drake has 416 tattooed on his right side as homage to his home city Toronto, and to Aaliyah. (see **Tattoo**)

Aston Martin Music

Aston Martin Music is the third single from Rick Ross' fourth studio album, Teflon Don, featuring Drake and Chrisette Michele. The song was well received by fans and critics, reaching number two on the US Billboard Hot R&B/Hip-Hop Songs and number one on the Billboard Rap Song charts. It was also certified gold with sales of 500,000 copies by the Recording Industry Association of America.

Drake released a similar song called Paris Morton Music, named after the American model Paris Morton, which does not feature either Ross or Michele.

- Released: 5 October 2010
- Album: Teflon Don
- Label: Maybach, Def Jam
- Length: 4:31
- Writers: Aubrey Graham, William Roberts, Chrisette Michele, Kevin Crowe, Erik Ortiz
- Producer: J.U.S.T.I.C.E League
- Music Video: Gil Green

The music video for Aston Martin Music which featured both Drake and Michele was directed by Gil Green and released on 23 October 2010.

Astrological Sign

Aubrey Drake Graham was born on 24 October 1986 in Toronto, Canada under the star sign of Scorpio. It is the eighth astrological sign in the Zodiac and spans 23 October to 21 November. Drake and a number of his friends have called themselves, October's Very Own or OVO for many years. He has also named his annual Toronto music festival the OVO Festival, and he takes astrology very seriously.

In the West, astrology often consists of a system of horoscopes that claim to explain aspects of a person's personality. It tries to predict future events in their life based on the positions of the sun, the moon, and other planetary objects at the time of their birth.

Scorpio is reputed to be the most powerful sign of the zodiac.

Scorpio facts:

Element	Water	Vibration	Resilient
Ruling planet	Pluto, Mars	Day	Tuesday
Symbol	The Scorpion	Lucky numbers	9, 18
Colour	Red, Scarlet	Flowers	Anemone
Birthstone	Bloodstone, Topaz	Metal	Iron, Steel
Life's Goal	To be greater than all opposition	Secret wish	To triumph

On his Room for Improvement mixtape, Drake includes a track called A Scorpion's Mind, featuring Nickelus F in an obvious nod to his astrological sign.

Avocado Supper Club

The Avocado Supper Club was situated on Adelaide St West and John Street and it was here that Drake played with his first band, The Renaissance. (see **Renaissance The**) The band played cover music three times a week in the basement of the club in 2005. The band – consisting of Drake, Melanie Fiona, Aion Clarke and Dalton Tennant – entertained the diners, playing mostly cover versions of popular songs of the day. Drake provided Master of Ceremony duties, entertaining the customers with his wise cracks and cheeky charm along with providing backing vocals and occasionally rapping a verse over Fiona and Clarke's vocals with Tennant on the keys.

The Avocado Supper Club eventually closed in 2008.

Away From Home Tour

In preparation for the release of his debut album Thank Me Later, Drake embarked on his first headlining tour of North America. The Away From Home tour, which was originally planned to run from 6 April through to 8 May 2010, followed his big break opening for Lil Wayne in the Young Money Presents: America's Most Wanted Music Festival the previous year. It was his first full-length performance since he fell and reinjured his right knee while on the Wayne tour, although he had appeared as a guest artist on numerous shows including Jay Z's Blueprint 3 tour in Toronto on 31 October 2009.

The tour featured opening performances from fellow Canadian rapper/singer k-os and the New York synth pop band, Francis & The Lights. Backed by a four-piece band and his DJ Future the Prince, Drake opened up on the first night at Slippery Rock University with Forever and shouted to the crowd 'I want this thing forever man.' His fans joined him on the first verse of Unstoppable, even drowning Drake out and he went on to perform the live premier of the much talked about song Fireworks at the show.

'I'm so excited to share this moment with you, because it's really my first show back in six months,' Drake told the excitable crowd. He then turned to his band saying: 'Take me somewhere please.' Later, Drake performed his string of collaborations such as Say Something and Bedrock, during which he gave an extra special tribute to Aaliyah. The recently incarcerated Lil Wayne was saluted during Best I Ever Had, Lust for Life and Houstatlantavegas which was followed by Over. As the encouraging crowd were participating and chanting he shouted out to them 'I'm doin' me, I'm doin' me' before eventually leaving the stage.

The shows in San Francisco, Los Angeles and Denver sold out in a matter of hours, and his Syracuse University show set a new attendance record of 9,500.

To raise eco-friendly awareness, Drake teamed up with the non-profit organisation Reverb, which set up Eco Village tents on campuses during the tour in the hope of educating college students about green technology and its uses. Drake also played his part by using biodiesel fuel, as well as biodegradable and recyclable products on the tour bus and backstage at his performances. The tour was therefore rightly dubbed the 'Campus Consciousness Tour.'

It was during the Away From Home tour that Drake first started using the services of vocal coach Dionne Osborne from Jan Smith Studios. (see **Vocal Coach**)

Away From Home Tour 2010 dates and locations:

April
04-05: Slippery Rock, PA. Slippery Rock University
04-06: Charleston, IL. Eastern Illinois University
04-07: Columbus, OH. Private location
04-09: State College, PA. Penn State University
04-10: Boston, MA. Private location
04-11: Lock Haven, PA. Private location
04-14: East Lansing, MI. Michigan State University
04-15: Rochester Hills, MI. Oakland University
04-16: Morganstown, WV. West Virginia University
04-20: Atlanta, GA. Havana Club
04-21: Orlando, FL. University Central Florida
04-22: Greenville, SC. Furman University
04-24: New Orleans, LA. New Orleans Jazz Festival
04-26: Kansas City, MO. University of Missouri
04-27: Lexington, KY. University of Kentucky
04-29: Lowell, MA. University Mass, Lowell
04-30: Syracuse, NY. Private location

May

05-01: East Rutherford, NJ. Bamboozle Festival
05-04: Worcester, MA. College of the Holy Cross
05-05: Baltimore, MD. Pier Six Concert
05-06: Cheney, PA. Towson University
05-07: Ithaca, NY. Cornell University
05-08: Plymouth, NH. Private location

During the tour on 20 April, Drake took part in the 13th Annual BMI Unsigned Urban Showcase, held at the Havana Club in Atlanta with acts from across America performing. The evening, in front of industry big-wigs was supposed to showcase Drake's talents but unfortunately everything didn't go to plan. Tickets were oversold for the evening, with the club became so overcrowded that he had to stand on top of the speakers to enable the fans to see him. This was followed by trouble with the microphone constantly tripping, which got so bad that he and Birdman had to share a microphone. To make matters worse Drake was unable to hear the music through his earpiece for the whole of his set, effectively leaving him unable to hear the beat. Disappointed, Drake addressed the crowd after his set and said somebody would be fired that night and apologised for the show which he likened to a High School talent show. He obviously didn't win the showcase.

Nearly a month into the tour on Monday 26 April, at the University of Missouri in Kansas City, Drake informed the crowd that later that night he would submit the final copy of his debut studio album, Thank Me Later. He claimed that the show would go down in history, not only because it was his first time in Kansas City, but also because it would be the city where the final cut of his first studio album would be turned in.

Due to the popular demand from his fans to the first half of the tour, which was originally scheduled to end in May, Drake added more dates in the US and Europe, with him finally ending the tour in Vancouver, Canada on 27July 2010.

Dates for the second leg of Drake's Away From Home tour:

May
05-20: Houston, TX. Verizon Wireless Theatre
05-21: Austin, TX. Stubbs
05-23: Memphis, TN. Cannon Center
05-25: Charlotte, NC. Fillmore
05-27: Cleveland, OH. House of Blues
05-28: Cincinnati, OH. Bogart's

June
06-03: Providence, RI. WWKX Hot Night
06-04: Hartford, CT. WZMX Hot Jam
06-05: Boston, MA. WJMN Summer Jam
06-06: New York, NY. Summer Jam Hot 97
06-07: Manchester, UK. MEN Arena
06-09: Birmingham, UK. LG Arena
06-12: St Louis, MO. WHHL Super Jam
06-13: Washington, DC. 9:30 Club
06-16: Philadelphia, PA. Filmore TLA Show
06-18: Seattle, WA. Kube 93 Summer Jam
06-19: Los Angeles, CA. Power 106 Powerhouse

July
07-02: Arendal, Norway. Hove Festival
07-03: Roskilde, Denmark. Roskilde Festival
07-04: London, UK. Wireless Festival
07-05: Paris, France. La Cigale
07 07: Amsterdam, Holland. Paradiso
07-08: Liege, Belgium. Les Ardentes Festival
07-09: Kildare, Ireland. Oxegen Festival

August
07-10: Kinross, UK. T in the Park
07-12: London, UK. Shepherd's Bush Empire
07-13: London, UK. Shepherd's Bush Empire
07-16: Ottawa, ON. Cisco Ottawa Bluesfest
07-17: St John's, NB. Harbour Station
07-18: Montreal, QC. Metropolis
07-21: Winnipeg, MB. Centennial Hall
07-23: Saskatoon, SK. Credit Union Centre
07-24: Edmonton, AB. Edmonton Events Centre
07-25: Calgary, AB. The Big 4
07-27: Vancouver, BC. Centre for Performing Arts

Drake opened for Jay Z at Manchester and Birmingham on the 7 and 9 June respectively, as part of the Blueprint 3 tour, but unfortunately had to postpone the following European legs of the tour due to his mother undergoing surgery on her spine and his wish to support her. He said at the time:

> 'Despite my best hopes, it is apparent that my mother will need surgery earlier than anticipated. In light of this news, I have made the difficult decision to cancel my European tour in order to support her during her recovery, just as she has supported me through the years. I cannot thank my European fans enough and look forward to performing abroad soon. I ask everyone to please respect my family's privacy during this time.'

After his mother's successful surgery, Drake returned to the Away From Home tour for the Canadian dates. The cancelled dates were eventually rescheduled for November of that year as part of the Light Dreams and Nightmares tour.

B

Bar Mitzvah

Raised by his mother in Forest Hill, a wealthy, predominately Jewish area of central Toronto, Drake has always taken his Jewish heritage seriously. He attended a Jewish day school and held his Bar Mitzvah party in the basement of an Italian restaurant in Toronto. Drake remembered that the song of the night was the Backstreet Boy's hit I Want It That Way and often jokes that his mother still has hopes of him marrying a nice Jewish girl. Bar Mitzvah is the Jewish coming of age ceremony and takes place when the boy reaches 13 and becomes a full-fledged member of the Jewish religion, with the responsibilities that comes with it. In May 2011, he performed at the Bar Mitzvah for the son of former NBC Chairman, Jeff Zucker, which was held in the Four Seasons Restaurant, New York. He allegedly picked up $250,000 for the 30-minute gig, at which he sung all his smash hits to the obvious delight of the guests. At the end of his set Drake gave an inspirational speech to the guest of honour.

> 'Tonight this is your moment. I want to let you know you're a man now. So I want to encourage you man, to make the right decisions. Pick your friends wisely, it seems like you got a lot of great people around you, that love you and I want you to take a lot of wisdom from the people in this room. To all my young Jewish men, keep being great Jewish men, I'm gonna' do the same.'

Drake has been photographed with a diamond studded Chai necklace, which is a symbol that figures prominently in Jewish culture. It has symbolic importance as an emblem meaning life and is considered a particularly lucky symbol. (see **Chai**)

Barnes Matt

UK-born Toronto photographer Matt Barnes first worked with Drake in 2005 after the two were introduced through Toronto's *Urbanology* magazine. He continued to work with the rapper until 2010 and shot the iconic 2007 Comeback Season mixtape cover picture.

Photographing since he was given a Minolta X-700 by his father at the age of 15, Barnes said:

> 'I'd stage shoots with my friends, and even then I'd enjoy making it into a production, propping and getting them dressed up for my camera. The next year at school I did a co-op placement with a photography studio and that really had me hooked. I doubt a week has gone by since I was given my first camera that I haven't taken a photo.'

Barnes is closely associated with Westside Studio, Canada's largest advertising and design photography facility and he released 5 years worth of Drake photographs through his 'tumblr' blog. The collection included numerous photographs, some of which have previously been published in various worldwide publications along with a number of unseen photographs.

Matt Barnes has generously given permission to use some of his photographs throughout this book and his contact details are below.

E:matt@thtsthespot.com   **W**:wwwthtsthespot.com

Basement

While he was in the sixth grade, Drake's family moved home to Coulson Avenue in Forest Hill, a wealthy suburb of Toronto. Drake lived in the basement of the house, which had its own living room and bedroom, while his mother and grandmother lived on the first floor. It was in this basement – which he fondly called the 'Blue Basement' – that Drake first started to write page after page of lyrics, rhymes and phrases in his notebooks. He eventually ended up filling numerous boxes with the collection of books and notepads, which he kept in his wardrobe thinking that they may come in handy sometime in the future. It was also in his basement room that he would try out his stage moves, conduct imaginary interviews and sing his rhymes into a microphone he had bought on eBay (see **eBay**) which he had set at the correct height for him to perform.

Drake wrote most of his verses and freestyles at a small circular table he had made, which featured images and photographs of all his musical heroes such as Barry White, Frank Sinatra, Stevie Wonder, Notorious B.I.G. and Pharrell.

Basketball

On 16 October 2009, Drake made an appearance at the Kentucky Wildcats men's basketball event, Big Blue Madness at the Rupp Arena, where head coach John Calipari had asked him to be a guest coach for the night. Since that night he has become a fan of the team and returns whenever his schedule allows. He has said he really connected with the college team who represent the University of Kentucky and that during his time there he bonded with several of the players who included John Wall, DeMarcus Cousins and Patrick Patterson.

Drake said of his involvement with the team:

> 'All of us really just bonded this year. I went to see a lot of
> the games last season. I'm also very close with Coach Cal,
> so I just showed my support. I took a lot of planes to see a
> lot of games.' he rhymed.

Drake had been spotted in the stands earlier that year for the Kentucky Wildcats versus Louisville game on 2 January, and afterwards he attended the post-game radio show as a guest of Coach Calipari.

On 15 September 2012, Drake returned to the University of Kentucky to once again coach a team for the annual charity game. During half-time along with Calipari, Drake presented a cheque for over $300,000 to local charities with the largest donation going to the local Kentucky recovery efforts after the recent tornado devastation. During the evening, Drake took the opportunity to thank the coach and the Wildcats for helping him develop a sense of belonging with the team, which he said had helped encourage him to finally complete his diploma.

Drake went on to narrate the Kentucky University Basketball documentary *Bluegrass Kingdom: The Gospel of Kentucky Basketball,* which aired on TruTV on Sunday 17 March 2013. During the hour-long documentary, Drake further explains his involvement with the team and his friendship with head coach John Calipari. The documentary showcased the team's basketball legacy and included interviews and first-hand reflections from a variety of former players, coaches and opponents.

Drake has performed twice at UKs Rupp Arena, on 27 April 2010 during his Away From Home – calling Calipari and the team on stage after the show – and again on Wednesday 22 February 2012 during his Club Paradise North America tour.

Drake is now such a big part of the 'Big Blue Nation' he received a customised championship ring commemorating the Wildcats 2012 NCAA title, engraved with the moniker 'Drizzy'.

On 30 September 2013, Drake became a 'global ambassador' for the Toronto Raptors, in the hope that his popularity can help boost the fading fortunes of his hometown basketball team. The club announced the move in the atrium of the Air Canada Center, along with the news that the Raptors will play host to the NBA all-star game in 2016, the first time the event will be held outside the US. Under the terms of the deal Drake, a keen Raptors fan and season ticket holder, will have input – along with Oliver El-Khatib – in the rebranding of the team colours, logo and all merchandising. Also look out for a Drake appearance at the 2016 all-star game as part of the half-time entertainment!

Bedrock

Bedrock is the second single by hip-hop group Young Money Entertainment, from their debut collaboration album, We Are Young Money. Originally debuting at number twenty six on the Billboard Hot 100, it eventually reached number two in March 2010 making it the most successful single by the group on the chart to date. The song went on to be the group's first top ten hit in the United Kingdom, peaking at number nine on 3 April 2010.

- Released: 14 November 2009
- Album: We Are Young Money
- Label: Young Money, Cash Money, Universal Republic
- Length: 4:48
- Writers: Wayne Carter Jr, Carl Lily, Aubrey Graham, Onika Maraj, Michael Stevenson, Jarvis Mills, Garrett
- Producer: Kane Beatz, Timbaland, Kanye West
- Music Video: Davo, Lil Wayne.

Best Day

Jay Z's Blueprint 3 North American tour touched down at Toronto's Air Canada Center on 31 October 2009. The sold-out crowd of more than 20,000 was in for a treat as the rap legend provided a memorable moment for Canadian hip-hop in general and Drake in particular.

Opening the show, recently signed Roc Nation artist J Cole, performed his Lights Please and Where You Going. Wale and N.E.R.D with Pharell Williams then worked the crowd into the groove, before Jay Z opened his spot with his smash hit Run This Town. Then with an inspirational aside to the packed crowd about the drive to succeed, he cued the instrumental to Successful, prompting immediate recognition from the crowd and a boisterous reception, as Drake strolled confidently onto the stage.

In his first concert appearance since he reinjured his knee in July – he last limped on stage for a quick cameo during Lil Wayne's Toronto show in August – the rapper delivered a laid-back performance of his hit song with Jay Z book-ending his verses with spot on ad-libs and the closest thing to a passing of the torch was experienced.

Drake said of the night:

> 'I'll never forget that night, as I looked into the eyes of forty odd people in the front rows. There were ex-girlfriends, guys who hated me, people who loved me, my mother was there and I remember thinking this is it.'

The after-show party was held at a Queens Street bar and Tyrone 'T-RexXx' Edwards, who organises Drake's Toronto parties when he's in town, remembered the night well.

He said:

> 'The budget has changed but the vibe is still the same; no paps or hangers on, just a select circle of good friend's looking for a good time, and the night was complete after the show when Jay Z took a turn mixing cocktails at the bar; it was a great Halloween night.'

Best I Ever Had

Best I Ever Had, is the first single from Drake's So Far Gone EP. The song, released on 13 February 2009, was written about an ex-girlfriend from Toronto and was taken from Drake's third mixtape of the same name.

- Released: 13 February (single)19 February 2009 (download)
- Album: So Far Gone EP
- Label: Young Money, Cash Money, Universal Motown
- Length: 4:19
- Writers: Aubrey Graham, Danny Hamilton, Matthew Samuels, Wayne Carter Jr, Nakia Coleman
- Producers: Boi-1da
- Music Video: Kanye West

Within two weeks of its availability for sale on iTunes, Best I Ever Had sold more than 300,000 copies and was the highest charting song ever by an unsigned artist, reaching number one after just nine weeks on the Hot R&B/Hip-Hop Song chart. This was the quickest progression to the top of the chart by a debuting artist since 2001, when Lil Romeo's first chart entry, My Baby reached the summit. It was the list's first independently distributed number one since Lil Jon's Snap Yo Fingers in 2006. The record also reached number one on the US Rap chart and number two on the US Hot 100 chart, behind the Black Eyed Peas hit I've Got a Feeling.

Best I Ever Had, which samples Fallin' in Love by Hamilton, Joe Frank & Reynolds, has been nominated for numerous awards:

- Two Grammy Award Nominations for Best Rap Solo Performance and Best Rap Song, but failed to win an award.
- Billboard's Hot Rap Song of the Year.
- The 2010 Most Performed Song by the American Society for Composers, Authors and Publishers.
- Nominated for Single of the Year at the 2010 Juno Awards, eventually losing out to Michael Buble's hit Haven't Met You Yet.

The concept for the music video came after a recording session involving Kanye West, Drake and Big Sean. After working through numerous scenarios for the video, West came up with the final vision for the basketball-themed video. Premiered on AMTV on 2 July 2009, the five minute video – directed by Kanye West – shows Drake coaching an all-female basketball team. Shot in Brooklyn, New York at the Bishop Ford Catholic High School, the video featured cameos from Trey Songz, Fabolous, Consequence and other Young Money Entertainment artist's along with the song's producer Boi-1da.

On 13 February 2013, the song was certified double platinum by the Recording Industry Association of America with sales of over 2 million copies.

In the United Kingdom, Best I Ever Had was released on 11 October 2010, as a double-A-side single with Fancy. Since debuting on iTunes, the track has sold more than 600,000 copies and has topped three separate music charts.

Billboard Music Awards

The Billboard Music awards are based on the year-end number of downloads, total airplay and sales according to the Nielsen Company's data on what consumers are currently buying and are sometimes viewed to be a more accurate way of judging the most popular songs of the year.

At the 2013 award ceremony, held on Sunday 19 May at the MGM Grand Arena, Las Vegas, Drake was nominated for three awards, losing out to his good friends, Justin Bieber for Best Male Artist and Nicki Minaj, who won the Top Streaming Artist and Top Rap Artist awards.

Since 2011, Drake has been nominated for twelve Billboard Music Awards in total without winning a single award.

BlackBerry

Drake types all his raps and verses onto his BlackBerry, as he finds it easier than writing them down with a pen and paper and he often jokes that his thumbs were made for a BlackBerry. He also uses his BlackBerry to scroll down the verses while he is rapping into the microphone when recording in the studio.

His producer Noah '40' Shebib has said he worries so much that Drake will misplace his BlackBerry, with all his verses on it that he has a number of BlackBerry's as back-up in the studio so that he will always have one to hand and he also ensures that he backs everything up.

Drake talks about putting his verses onto his BlackBerry on the track, Say What's Real from his So Far Gone mixtape. He suggests to the finder of his BlackBerry he had lost while on holiday at Cabo San Lucas in Mexico, to sell it on to a rapper because the verses will be worth a fortune.

Drake has said his BlackBerry is the one piece of modern technology he can't do without. BlackBerry, a Canadian company has also sponsored Drake's OVO Festival which is held in Toronto every year.

Black Entertainment Television (BET)

The Black Entertainment Television Awards were established in 2001 by the Black Entertainment Television network, to celebrate African-American, and other minorities in music, acting, sports and entertainment. Drake has been nominated 27 times for a BET award, winning on six occasions, including for Best Male Hip-Hop Artist Award twice in successive years 2010-11 and as part of the Young Money collective, winning the Best Group award in 2011.

Drake has performed live at the awards on two occasions, at the 2010 awards ceremony, backed by his band he performed the first verse of Fireworks in a melody with Over before bringing Young Jeezy onto the stage for the duo to perform a remix of his hit Lose My Mind. In 2011 he performed I'm On One with Lil Wayne, DJ Khaled and Rick Ross. (see **Photographs**)

At the 2013 ceremony, held at the Nokia Theatre in Los Angeles on 30 June, Drake won a further two awards – from five nominations – for Video of the Year and Viewers Choice with Started From the Bottom.

Blackstone Adam

Adam Blackstone is an acclaimed multi-instrumentalist producer, songwriter and bass player in Drake's band. He was also the musical director on his 2011 Light Dreams and Nightmares tour. Blackstone has built up an enviable reputation in the music industry since he started playing drums with his father's band aged eight.

Multi-talented and able to play numerous instruments, he formed BASSic Black Entertainment in 2007 as a broad music-based company that specialises in live music production, artist development and studio production. Clients include Chris Brown, Eminem, John Legend and Kanye West. He has also been the musical director for Justin Timberlake's first nationally televised comeback performance with the single, Suit and Tie.

Blackstone performed with Drake, Eminem and Lil Wayne at the 2010 Grammy Award ceremony and has recently worked as musical director with Maroon 5, Nicki Minaj and Rihanna's 2012 tour 777. He continues to play a major part in Drake's music performances.

Blueprint 3

Blueprint 3 is the 11th studio album by American rapper Jay Z, which was released on 8 September 2009 on the Roc Nation label. The album which featured Kanye West and Rihanna, debuted at number one on the US Billboard 200 chart and was certified platinum by the RIAA with sales of over 1 million. Drake featured on the album with Off That the song he co-wrote with Jay Z. The album also includes the hit single Empire State of Mind, sung by Alicia Keys and featuring Jay.

Drake appeared on the Toronto leg of the Blueprint 3 tour to promote the album at the Air Canada Center on 31 October 2009, performing his song Successful. He also appeared later during the tour with Lil Wayne and Nicki Minaj as surprise guests on 2 March 2010 at Madison Square Garden in New York, with each performing a verse off the single, I'm Goin' In with Drake breaking the night's all-black dress code by wearing white. He also opened the show in Manchester and Birmingham on 7 and 9 June respectively, later that year.

BMI Urban Award

The Broadcast Music Inc (BMI), founded in 1939, is one of the three United States performing rights organisations, along with ASCAP and SESAC that collects and distributes license fees on behalf of songwriters, composers and publishers as royalties. In 2012 Drake won the BMI Urban Award for Songwriter of the Year for the second year in succession. He also tied with Lil Wayne for the Most Performed Song of the Year, with seven songwriting credits, some of which they co-wrote.

The seven songs that earned Drake the 2012 award are as follows:

- Aston Martin Music
- Headlines
- I'm On One
- Moment 4 Life
- Right Above It
- She Will
- What's My Name

The event was held on Friday 7 September 2012, in Los Angeles and although Drake was not in attendance himself, Birdman and Tyler Williams picked up the award on his behalf.

In 2013, Drake left BMI and joined ASCAP, who already represented his long-time producers Noah Shebib and Boi-1da. (see **ASCAP**).

Boi-1da

After years of slaving away over his Acer laptop in the basement of his family's home, to producing _the_ song of summer 2009, Matthew 'Boi-1da' Samuels has certainly come a long way, since his family moved to Ajax, Toronto when he was five years old from their home in Jamaica. In 2006, he was introduced to Drake by high school friend and fellow producer, Dalton 'D10' Tennant who had played keyboard with Drizzy in his first band, The Renaissance. Since then, Boi-1da has gone on to work on all three of Drake's mixtapes and three studio albums to date, including producing the smash hit, Best I Ever Had, from the gold certified So Far Gone EP. Boi-1da remembers the first song that Drake had sent him:

'He was rapping about money, but not like anyone else would. It was so relatable his voice flow was crazy, I saw the vision from there and that first song was called Money.' Boi-1da was involved in producing three tracks from Drake's first mixtape, Room for Improvement in 2006, two from the Comeback Season mixtape, before striking gold with his production for the hit single, Best I Ever Had from Drake's third mixtape So Far Gone. He also produced The N Soundtrack Album for the American television channel Nickelodeon, released in August 2006 which featured Drake's first recorded single, Do What You Do. (see **The N Soundtrack**)

Boi-1da's profile has grown alongside that of Drake's especially after he produced the lead singles from two of the hottest albums of 2010. Over from Drake's first studio album, Thank Me Later – which was the eighth highest-selling album of the year – and Not Afraid from Eminem's comeback and the year's best-selling album, Recovery. Not Afraid debuted at number one on the Billboard Hot 100 and the video, directed by Richard Lee, has had an astronomical 435,488,077 hits on YouTube, as of September 2013.

Using the FL Studio 9 music-production system and a laptop as his main equipment of choice, Boi-1da has also co-produced with Noah '40' Shebib, the platinum selling hit Headlines from Drake's second studio album Take Care, which was released on Young Money Entertainment and Cash Money Record labels. (see **Photographs**)

Winning two Grammy Awards for Best Rap Solo Performance with Eminem's Not Afraid and Best Rap Album for Eminem's comeback album Recovery from a total of five nominations at the 2011 Grammy Awards, it was a far cry from the day he bought his first ever CD...Eminem's Slim Shady LP in February 1999.

In 2013 he was rewarded for his co-production skills for the single, Headlines from Drake's Take Care, when the album won a Grammy Award for Best Rap Album.

Bria's Interlude

American model Bria Myles, was the inspiration behind Bria's Interlude, a track from Drake's So Far Gone mixtape, which featured American R&B singer Omarion. Bria's Interlude did not make the final cut for the seven-track So Far Gone EP, which was released in September 2009. Drake said of the song: 'I was smitten with this girl from LA and I started writing a song for her.'

Bryant Cortez

Cortez Bryant is the New York based CEO of Bryant Management and has managed Drake since July 2009. He is one of the most influential and successful businessmen in the music industry today and is one of the chief visionaries behind Young Money Entertainment.

Bryant has been a mentor to Lil Wayne since they both attended Eleanor Mc Main Secondary School in New Orleans – Bryant, three years ahead of Wayne – with the two becoming close while playing in the school's cymbal band. This was after Bryant, who led the band, had organised a practice session at his home, with Wayne being the only member of the band to turn up. He has also held the role as Wayne's financial adviser after Wayne had left the Hot Boy's group to become a single rapper. After accepting the role, Bryant accompanied Wayne on tour for a couple of years, doing numerous jobs from roadie to DJ, before finally becoming his manager in 2003.

In 2005, Lil Wayne was named President of Cash Money, founding Young Money Entertainment as a Cash Money imprint however, by 2007 the increasingly busy Wayne had stepped down from heading both labels, handing the management duties of Young Money over to Bryant with Mack Maine as co-president.

Bryant first heard about Drake when Jas Prince, the son of Rap-A-Lot Records CEO James Prince, played him the CD of Comeback Season. He remembers thinking at the time:

> 'Wow, this guy. I can understand everything he is saying and his music feels so real. Then when we flew him in, and I met him, it was like, Oh wow this guy's a star. His personality just rubbed off and I could tell that he was a genuinely good person and would be a good addition to the Young Money team.'

While they keep separate staff, offices and clients for the rest of the business, Bryant Management has worked closely with Hip Hop Since 1978 – operated by rap moguls Yambol 'Hip-Hop' Joshua and Gee Roberson – to collectively manage Lil Wayne and Drake. (see **Photographs**)

Hip Hop Since 1978, have a good stable of artists including Atlanta rapper Young Jeezy, T.I and Drake's producer Noah '40' Shebib. For the last seven years Bryant has certainly managed his roster of artists well, with Lil Wayne completing 78 headlining shows in nine months in 2009, grossing well over $40 million, making him one of the most profitable touring artists. Similarly through his management skills, Drake has secured lucrative endorsement/sponsorship deals with big-name brands ranging from Sprite and Kodak to AT&T. Bryant, Gee Roberson and Lil Wayne all executive produced Drake's first two studio albums.

In April 2012, Bryant returned to Jackson State University – where he was a member of the University Jackson Marching Band – to donate $500,000 on behalf of retiring band director Dr Lewis Liddell, whom Bryant regarded as an inspiration while he attended the university on a band scholarship. Also that year he joined forces with Gee Roberson to form the Blueprint Group, a management and artist development group.

'Bubbe' Evelyn Sher

Drake's maternal grandmother, Evelyn Sher lived with Drake and his mother for a number of years until unfortunately she had to move into a nursing home during the last few years of her life. Affectionately called 'Bubbe' by Drake – the Yiddish name for grandmother – the two had a close bond and he used to teach her some of his early rap verses.

Evelyn has appeared, or has been mentioned in a number of Drake's songs, The Resistance, from his debut studio album Thank Me Later, with Drake, in a period of guilt-ridden reflection raps about his grandmother being in a nursing home with him not calling her.

He did visit his grandmother at the nursing home soon after signing his lucrative record deal while filming the 2010 MTV documentary *Drake: Better than Good Enough*. During one scene, while having a tender moment with his grandmother, he informs her that he had just signed a multi-million dollar record deal and asks her what she would have now that he could buy her anything in the world. She replies 'Just a kiss and a hug,' with Drake bending down to gently kiss her forehead. In an unreleased song called The Winner, he again talks about his grandmother.

On his 2011 song, Look What You've Done, from his Take Care album, Drake makes it a family affair, toasting his mother in the first verse, his uncle in the second and on the hook, Evelyn tells her grandson via voicemail from the nursing home of her memories of the good times they have had together and that she hopes to see him soon. She also appeared in a cameo role for the spoof sitcom, Us & Them starring and produced by Drake's good friend Al Mukadam. The 14-minute feature, also starring Drake and Uncle Steve, sees Drake auditioning for an acting role, buying a car and playing basketball, with some questionable camera work and dialogue.

Sadly, Evelyn Sher passed away on Thanksgiving Day 2011.

C

Cadastre Noel

While working at Metalworks Recording Studios in Ontario, Canada, Noel Cadastre was asked to work a late shift and assist Noah Shebib in finishing four songs that were still incomplete for Drake's upcoming album. Unfortunately, the duo began to run out of time due to Drake's upcoming Away From Home tour, so Cadastre was asked if he would go on the road to assist '40' in finishing the album that was to become Thank Me Later. Cadastre agreed and took two week's vacation from the studio to go on the road with Drake and the team. The two weeks became three and his vacation became permanent when '40', who had admired his work ethic, asked him to join the team, with Drake revealing to the crowd at the University of Missouri, Kansas on 26 April 2010 that he had submitted the final copy of the album.

Now Assistant Engineer to Shebib, Noel Cadastre's role involves assisting the recording and production work in the studio and liaising with the record label, with him and Shebib the only two people who record Drake's music. He has said that one of his best memories of his time working with Drake was recording in the studio called 'Marvin's Room' in LA, famous for being Marvin Gaye's old recording studio.

Calipari John

One of the more controversial figures in college and professional basketball, John Calipari has earned a fearsome reputation for being one of the best recruiters in college basketball, and noted for being able to turn average teams into championship-winning contenders.

Since April 2009, he has been the head coach of the Kentucky Wildcats men's basketball team. Born in Moon Township, Pennsylvania in 1959, Calipari studied at the University of North Carolina at Wilmington, where he was a two year letterman. He transferred to Clarion University and graduated with a bachelor's degree in marketing. He went on to play two years as a point guard at Clarion, before making the switch to coaching. Calipari is well known for his relentless recruitment of high school basketball prospects, and more often than not persuading them to join his team.

Somewhat unusually, Calipari has strong links to the music industry and includes artists such as Drake and Jay Z as friends. After the Kentucky Wildcats advanced to the 2011 Final Four (NCAA Division I) Jay Z was famously fined $50,000 by the NCAA for visiting the Wildcats locker room. The incident was included in the lyrics to the Jay Z and Kanye West's Grammy Award winning collaboration Ni**as in Paris. He also has a close personal friendship with Drake, who has been a regular visitor to the University of Kentucky ever since he was invited to be guest coach at the 'Big Blue Madness' event, held at the University's 23,000 seat Rupp Arena in October 2009. The annual pre-season practice game usually sells out within hours of the tickets going on sale. (see **Basketball**)

Since then, Drake has been a regular visitor to watch the Wildcats after feeling what he described as an overwhelming connection with the team. Drake has said that Calipari's openness in inviting him to UK gave him a 'sense of love and a sense of belonging to something.' It was this sense of belonging that Drake has credited John Calipari and the team as being one of the inspirations, along with his mother for him finally graduating in 2012, at the age of 25. Calipari has been named National Coach of the Year three times and in 2012 led Kentucky to its 8th NCAA Tournament Championship and his first.

Carino 'Niko' Nicholas

When Drake was 16 and still acting on *Degrassi: The Next Generation,* he started to distribute his early mixtapes in Toronto clubs. It was on one of these promotion nights that he met his good friend 'Niko'. Nicholas Carino's team were promoting on one side of the club and Drake was working the other side and after reaching an agreement not to work on each other's patch they became good friends. Niko then decided that an easier way to meet and chat up girls was by giving away Drake's Room for Improvement mixtapes rather than selling tickets. Drake remembers going outside the club to grab some air and seeing Niko hustling with a group of clubbers, saying that this tape is the best and this guy will be the next best thing and really promoting him. It was this enthusiasm and his dedication that sparked their friendship and they have been inseparable ever since.

Nicholas Carino was born in Toronto and is of Filipino descent. A quiet bespectacled dude, it was Niko who shouted a warning when Drake was involved in an armed robbery in 2009. After visiting Vivoli's restaurant in Toronto, he was walking to his car with a female friend when two armed men told him to hand over his watch and money. Niko – who was a little way behind Drake – shouted out at the thieves and they immediately ran off with their haul. The two alleged assailants were picked up later by the Police and after prosecution they were jailed.

Drake credits Niko on his Thank Me Later sleeve credits as the 'brother he never had.' Niko has said of Drake:

> 'Everybody knows Drake isn't hood, Toronto rap used to be more street-oriented with Offishall, Saukrates and Choclair, the big names. But Drake came and flipped it and started saying everything that a hood guy couldn't say. I guess that's why people like him.'

It was Niko or Neeks, as the OVO crew call him, whom Drake credits for encouraging him to get his afro cut by J-Mac, a Toronto barber. After getting his haircut, Drake stated that his life changed forever. (see **J-Mac**)

Cash Money Records

Cash Money Records is a subsidiary of the Universal Music Group and was founded by brothers Bryan 'Birdman' and Ronald 'Slim' Williams in the early 1990s and along with producer Mannie Fresh, they are recognised as building the unique sound of Cash Money Records.

After moderate early success, the label signed Lil Wayne's group, The Hot Boys, who went on to become the label's main artists, along with the rapper Juvenile. In 1998 after years of moderate success, Cash Money signed a lucrative distribution and pressing deal with Universal Records and Juvenile's multi-platinum selling album, 400 Degreez soon followed. In 2007, Wayne became President of Cash Money Records, but stepped down soon afterwards to be replaced by his friend and manager Cortez Bryant, with Wayne returning to his music career.

In 2009, Cash Money Records took part in a bidding war for Drake's signature before signing him in a joint venture with Aspire and Young Money Entertainment with distribution through Universal. Other notable Cash Money artists include Nicki Minaj, DJ Khaled, Tyga, Mac Maine and of course Lil Wayne himself.

In July 2013, Cash Money and Young Money released their first compilation album called Rich Gang. The album contained contributions from Lil Wayne, Nicki Minaj, Tyga and Mack Maine, along with outside artists such as Rick Ross and Future, but unfortunately Drake was too busy working on his third studio album, Nothing Was the Same to figure on the album.

The first single from the album, Tapout which featured Wayne, Nicki Minaj, Future and Mack Maine, was released to moderate success.

Chai

Drake often wears a diamond encrusted Chai necklace, which he was photographed wearing for the cover of Vibe magazine in 2009. Chai is a Hebrew word and symbol that figures prominently in Jewish culture. The symbol has special importance due to its appearance in the Hebrew slogan 'The people of Israel live!' and is one of the most recognizable symbols of Judaism. Each Hebrew letter also has a numerical value and Chai comprises the words chet (8) and yud (10). Therefore, the word Chai adds up to eighteen, which is considered very lucky and gifts are sometimes given in multiples of eighteen.

Chambers Christopher

In 2006, Christopher Chambers founded the New York based media publicity company, The Chamber Group (TCG). TCG have a close working relationship with Bryant Management and looks after their main stars, including Drake, Lil Wayne, Tyga and Birdman. Their main area of expertise is public relations, image branding and regulating media access to their roster of artists, especially while the team is on the road touring. They aid publicity signings, album release parties and tour venue publicity. They were responsible for the publicity surrounding Lil Wayne's hugely profitable I Am Still Music Tour in 2008-9.

The Group arranged the release and listen party for Drake's album, Thank Me Later on Tuesday 15 June 2010, at 5 Ninth New York for music critics and media outlets.

Champagne

One of Drake's favourite drinks is champagne, such as Krug Rose and Dom Perignon Rose and he has always had an ambition to start his own champagne company, or to be associated with an already established business.

Chase N. Cashe

Jesse Woodard, aka Chase N. Cashe, is an American hip-hop recording artist and producer from New Orleans. Working out of Los Angeles, he has produced hits for several artists including Eminem, Pussycat Dolls, Lil Wayne and Drake. Meeting Drake in Atlanta in 2009, the duo kept in touch and Cashe co-produced the single, Look What You've Done, from the Take Care album with Noah Shebib. Cashe the hip-hop artist also opened for Drake on the first leg of his 2012 Club Paradise tour of North America and said of his time on the tour:

> 'I enjoyed meeting the fans, passing out my music and taking cues from Drake, Kendrick Lamar and A$AP Rocky. It was priceless performing in front of sold out shows every night.'

Cashe has been in the music industry since a teenager when he and his partner Hit-Boy, under the beat master Polow Da Don, developed Surf Club Productions. He released his debut mixtape Gumbeaux, in April 2011 and quickly followed up with The Heir Up There, which was released while Chase was touring with Drake on the Club Paradise tour.

Cherry Beach Sound

Cherry Beach Sound is a recording studio based in Toronto, Ontario. Founded in 1982, the studio have played host to an impressive roster of musicians who have recorded there, including John Legend, 50 Cent, Timbaland, Wyclef Jean, Trey Songz and of course, Drake. Drake completed his second studio album, Take Care at the studio, with the Cherry Beach management team posting the following on their website:

> 'We are happy to welcome Canadian hip-hop producer Noah '40' Shebib and Young Money/Cash Money Records for the completion of Drake's second full studio album Take Care. The album is scheduled for release 15 November 2011.'

Clarke 'Voyce' Aion

Aion Clarke is a singer-songwriter from Toronto, Ontario. He has known Drake from their teenage days in Toronto when they performed together in Drake's first band, The Renaissance at the Avocado club. The foursome played popular cover songs of the day, with Clarke backing Melanie Fiona on vocals, while Drake rapped a few verses and was Master of Ceremonies for the night. After the band disbanded, Clarke went solo with his blend of pop, soul and big band swing numbers, but he continued to collaborate with Drake, appearing on the songs, All This Love and Special from his debut 2006 mixtape, Room for Improvement.

Clarke has gone on to carve out a successful career for himself since leaving The Renaissance and has penned a number of smash hits for other artists, such as Dem Haters for Rihanna, and Got Me Going for the American R&B group Day 26, his first US Billboard Hot 100 entry in 2008.

Clarke was privileged to sing the Canadian National Anthem on the Saturday of the 2011 NBA All Star Entertainment Series weekend in Los Angeles, where he was reunited with the other original members of The Renaissance. (see **Renaissance The**)

Clarke also appeared with Drake on the Young Artists for Haiti campaign single Wavin Flag, to help the people of Haiti after the devastation caused by the earthquake, in 2010.

Clinton Bill

On 17 March 2011, Drake joined former US President Bill Clinton at Boulevard 3, 6523 Sunset Boulevard, Hollywood for the Clinton Foundation's Millennium Network fundraising event. The Foundation focuses on everything from climate change to education and caring for HIV sufferers, with a mission statement to improve global health, strengthen economies and promote healthier lifestyles. Drake who co-hosted the evening with the former President took to the stage and performed a six-song set to close the night after Clinton had spoken the closing remarks to the assembled audience. During his speech, Clinton gave an explanation of the Foundation's aims and his efforts to encourage students and young activists to get involved in global issues such as obesity, economic development and climate change around the world. Drake said of the event:

> 'One of my favourite pictures in my house is of me and Bill and I'm wearing a zebra Supreme jacket and he's wearing a suit, its wild!'

Clipse

Clipse is an American hip-hop group formed by brothers Gene 'Malice' and Terence 'Pusha T' Thornton in Virginia in 1992. After being introduced to Pharell Williams, Williams signed the duo to Aristra records through his Star Trak Entertainment Label and he went on to produce their 2002 debut album Lord Willin', which was certified gold with sales of over 500,000 by the RIAA. It was the association with Pharell and Star Trak that brought Clipse to Drake's attention – due to Pharell being one of his early hip-hop heroes – and he started to follow their career closely.

When Drake was a teenager he bought a microphone off eBay for $200, because it had allegedly been signed by 'Pusha T' who was one of his favourite hip-hop stars at that time. After he purchased the microphone, he set it up in the basement at home and would use it to practice his verses and dummy interviews. He used it so much that the signature eventually wore away, and to this day he still does not know if the signature was authentic. 'Malice' featured on Do What You Do from Drake's 2007 mixtape, Comeback Season.

Clothing Line

Drake has always taken great efforts to establish a unique brand with his music, his look and the cloths that he wears, largely influenced by his brand manager and former Ransom clothing buyer, stylist and designer Oliver El-Khatib. (see **Khatib-El**) The duo eventually decided to introduce their own clothing line, opening the October's Very Own online clothing store in 2010. The store has Drake's 'You Only Live Once' motto and the OVO owl or OVO logo emblazoned onto t-shirts, jackets, hoodies and sweatshirts amongst the range.

Drake says of the brand:

'I want to give the fans a product and a piece of myself, I love it when I see some of the fans with an OVO jacket or owl sweatshirts.'

In 2010 Drake designed just three special-edition red OVO jackets by Canadian clothing line Roots, presenting one each to Lil Wayne and Birdman keeping the third for himself. The personalised jackets featured; the Thank Me Later and So Far Gone titles on the chest, Young Money, Cash Money, ATF, and HHS78 logos down the left arm with the flying angel and the words Away From Home down the right. The Canadian and American flags made up the logos on the jacket with 5 stars on the back. Drake wore his jacket for the first time on the Miss Me video and again during the Light Dreams and Nightmares tour at the Houston Reliant Arena on 29 October 2010. He later held a competition on the AllThings-Fresh.net website giving the jacket away to a member of his fan club.

Drake teamed up again with Roots when he designed a limited edition OVO varsity jacket. The jackets, costing $500 sold exclusively in only two stores world-wide, in Toronto at Nomad and in New York at Nepenthes. For the launch in New York on 5 November 2011, fans camped outside the Nepenthes store for over 17 hours for the official release of the OVO tour jackets. Drake attended the opening and mingled with the fans having photographs taken and signing autographs.

Drake has also designed a luxury $5000 limited edition OVO Chilliwack coat for Canada Goose. The coat featured a buffalo leather exterior, removable artic fox-fur trim on the hood and a silk-lined interior. He was pictured wearing the coat while performing in Times Square New York, on New Year's Eve 2012.

Club Paradise Tour

The 2012 Club Paradise Tour was Drake's second headlining tour and he played a total of 65 shows in North America and Europe. The tour, in support of his album Take Care, was announced in October 2011, with dates confirmed in December that year. The first leg of the tour saw Drake performing at college arenas supported by A$AP Rocky and Kendrick Lamar, with him explaining that he wanted to go back to the college arenas that had supported him in the early days of his career:

> 'I fought for this tour, I fought really hard for this tour because my management wanted to go and get the big bucks, to go into the stadiums and cash out. But I really made this album for the same people that supported me since day one.'

American (1) Club Paradise Tour Venues

February
02-14: Miami, FL. Bank United Center
02-15: Gainesville, FL. Stephen C O'Connell Center
02-17: Nashville, TN. Bridgestone Arena
02-18: Columbus, OH. Schottenstein Center
02-21: Columbia, SC. Colonial Life Arena
02-22: Lexington, KY. Rupp Arena
02-24: Tallahassee, FL. Tallahassee-Leon County Center
02-25: New Orleans, LA. UNO Lakefront Arena
02-27: Austin, TX. Frank Erwin Center
02-28: Oklahoma City, OK. Chesapeake Energy Center

March
03-01: Kansas City, MO. Sprint Center
03-02: Arlington, TX. College Park Center
03-04: Tucson, AZ. Tucson Arena
03-05: Los Angeles, CA. Galen Center
03-07: Davis, CA. The Pavilion at ARC

March continued:
03-08: Fresno, CA. Save Mart Center
03-10: San Jose, CA. Event Center
03-11: San Diego, CA. Viejas Arena

European Club Paradise Tour Venues

Supporting Drake on selected UK and European legs of the tour were British artist Rita Ora, who sang Drake's song R.I.P. English rapper Tinie Tempah and English singer-songwriter Labrinth.

During the tour at the Birmingham LG Arena on 19 April, Drake fell on stage, immediately raising fears he had repeated his fall when he toured with Lil Wayne on the America's Most Wanted tour in 2009, when he damaged his knee which required surgery. (see **America's Most Wanted Tour**) Luckily he didn't hurt himself this time and perfected an awesome back-flip roll to return to a standing position and carried on singing Take Care to great applause.

March
03-24: Dublin, Ireland. The O2
03-26: London, England. The O2 Arena
03-27: London, England. The O2 Arena
03-29: Sheffield, England. Motorpoint Arena
03-30: Cardiff, Wales. Motorpoint Arena

April
04-01: Manchester, England. Manchester Arena
04-02: Glasgow, Scotland. Scottish Exhibition Center
04-05: Paris, France. Palais Omnisports De Paris
04-07: Brussels, Belgium. Forest National
04-08: Amsterdam, Holland. Heineken Music Hall
04-10: Frankfurt, Germany. Jahrhunderthalle
04-12: Berlin, Germany. Max Schmeling-Halle
04-13: Copenhagen, Denmark. Valby-Hallen
04-15: Stockholm, Sweden. Ericsson Globe

April continued:
04-16: Oslo, Norway. Oslo Spektrum
04-19: Birmingham, England. LG Arena
04-20: Birmingham, England. LG Arena
04-22: Liverpool, England. Echo Arena
04-23: Newcastle, England. Metro Radio Arena
04-25: Nottingham, England. Capital FM Arena

Supporting him on the American second leg of the tour were, 2 Chainz, J Cole, Waka Flocka Flame and French Montana. Drake said of the extended tour:

> 'I feel this tour is coming at the perfect time, taking place in the season that we all wait for. We're outdoors and you've got every single artist you want to hear in the club on one bill...that's Club Paradise.'

American (2) Club Paradise Tour Venues

May
05-07: Concord, CA. Sleep Train Pavilion
05-08: Irvine, CA. Verizon Wireless Amphitheatre
05-10: Phoenix, AZ. Ashley Furniture Home Store
05-11: Las Vegas, CA. MGM Grand Garden Arena
05-13: Denver, CO. Comfort Dental Amphitheatre
05-14: Albuquerque, NM. Hard Rock Casino
05-16: Dallas, TX. Gexa Energy Pavilion
05-17: Houston, TX. Toyota Center
05-19: Charlotte, NC. Verizon Wireless
05-20: Atlanta, GA. Aaron Amphitheatre at Lakewood
05-22: Raleigh, NC. Time Warner Cable Music Pavilion
05-23: Virginia Beach, VA. Farm Bureau
05-25: Washington, DC. Verizon Center
05-26: Pittsburg, PA. First Niagara Pavilion
05-28: Cleveland, OH. Blossom Music Center
05-30: Detroit, MI. DTE Energy Music Theatre

June
06-01: Indianapolis, IN. Klipsch Music Center
06-02: Chicago, IL. First Midwest Bank Amphitheatre
06-05: Memphis, TN. FedEx Forum
06-06: Cincinnati, OH. Riverbend Music Center
06-08: Darien Lake, NY. Darien Lake Arts Center
06-09: Philadelphia, PA. Susquehanna Bank Center
06-11: Hartford, CN. Comcast Center
06-12: Holmdel, NJ. PNC Bank Arts Center
06-14: Saratoga Springs, NY. Saratoga Arts Center
06-16: Long Island, NY. Nikon Theatre
06-17: Boston, MS. Comcast Center

Drake delivered an unforgettable show on the penultimate night of the tour at New York's Nikon at Jones Beach Theatre. With Meek Mill, Waka Flocka Flame and J Cole opening the show, Drake stepped onto the stage to start his own set with Lord Knows followed by collaborations with The Weeknd on Crew Love and 2 Chainz on No Lie. Then in a homage to New York hip-hop, rising stars A$AP Rocky and French Montana hit the stage followed by legendary Harlem group Dipset and Busta Rymes. Drake had called in all his favours to give the sold-out crowd a great show.

Finishing on 17June at the Comcast Center, Massachusetts the tour was the most successful hip-hop tour of 2012, grossing over $42 million.

Comeback Season

Comeback Season was Drake's second mixtape and according to some of his fans, the best of the three he has released. The free-to-download tape was released on 1 January 2007 on the October's Very Own label and consisted of a mixture of songs, freestyles and raps.

The mixtape sampled songs, Teach U A Lesson by Robin Thicke, Barry Bonds by Kanye West and ended with Drake free-styling over Brisco and Flo Rider's Man of The Year featuring Lil Wayne. Matthew 'Boi-1da' Samuels and Tyler 'T-Minus' Williams shared production duties with Drake's Manager, Terral Slack. The mixtape spawned one single, Replacement Girl, featuring Trey Songz, with the music video featuring on BET's New Joint of the Day on 30 April 2007, making Drake the first unsigned Canadian rapper to appear on the show.

Coming Out Show

In front of 300 invited guests, who included some of the biggest names in the music industry, Drake played at the *Hot 97 Who's Next show*, at SOB's in New York on 26 May 2009. The famous New York club has long been acknowledged as a rite of passage in hip-hop, with some career-defining performances having taken place there. For his show, Drake had all the music industry's big guns in the audience including Warner Atlantic boss Lyor Cohen, Ryan Leslie, Kanye West and representatives from Def Jam and MTV.

Bun B made a surprise appearance to join Drizzy on stage during his 30-minute set, which was positively reviewed in the *Rolling Stone* magazine and The *New York Times*. The *Rolling Stone* magazine called him 'the hottest MC in the game and a 22 year old prodigy.' The show was the last of his So far Gone Tour. (see **Photographs**)

Drake said of the show:

> 'When I was at SOB's it was a lot of nerves, not only that but it just had so much pressure behind the show, and I had no band. I still didn't have a sense of what it takes to make a great performance.'

59

He didn't need to worry as in July 2009, after one of the biggest bidding wars ever, Drake signed his lucrative recording deal with Aspire/Young Money/Cash Money and to be distributed by Universal. (see **Record Deal**)

Cosmopolitan's Marquee Nightclub

Drake spent the weekend of 22-23 October 2010, in Los Angeles to celebrate his 25th birthday and also to publicise the release of his Take Care album on 24 October, Drake's birthday. But due to contractual problems in having certain samples cleared, his management team decided to delay the album's release until 15 November 2010.

On 22 October Drake spent the night at the TAO nightclub at the Venetian Hotel, buying everybody in the bar shots and generally having a good time with his OVO crew. The following night the party continued and moved on to the Boom Box, a private room at the Cosmopolitan Marquee Club. The night was attended by a line-up of the great and good of the music industry. Along with Drake's friends from Toronto who included Oliver El-Khatib, producers Boi-1da and Tyler 'T-Minus' Williams, Jas Prince – who introduced his music to Lil Wayne – the CEO of Cash Money Records Bryan Williams, Lil Wayne, Hip Hop Since 1978 co-founder Gee Roberson, Young Money President Mack Maine and Drake's manager Cortez Bryant were also in attendance.

Crew Love

- Released: 2 October 2010
- Album: Take Care
- Label: Young Money, Cash Money, Universal Republic
- Length: 3:29
- Writers: A Graham, Abel Tesfaye, C Montagnese
- Producers: Noah Shebib, Illangelo, The Weeknd

Crew Love is the sixth single from Drake's second studio album, Take Care, and features guest vocals from fellow Toronto native The Weeknd, who also wrote and co-produced the track. Drake's creative director Oliver El-Khatib had introduced Drake to The Weeknd's music through playing his first mixtape, House of Balloons to him while driving together in Toronto. (see **The Weeknd**) After listening to the mixtape, Drake liked his vocals so much that he contacted him to arrange a meeting, with Crew Love becoming their first collaboration.

D

Dalton 'D10' Tennant

Dalton 'D10' Tennant, is a Toronto-based producer and musician who has played keyboards for Drake since 2005 when he played in Drake's first band, The Renaissance. Tennant is an accomplished organist who started playing the organ from an early age, playing for church services and the adult and youth choirs at his local church.

In 2006, Tennant formed his company Dee Tenn Productions, a production and management company based in Toronto. It was around this time that Tennant introduced his friend Boi-1da to Drake, who eventually went on to produce the smash hit Best I Ever Had. Drake has said it was '40', 'D10' and Boi-1da who really helped him define his sound.

Tennant has also been credited with writing and production on a number of Drake songs including, Brand New and Sooner Than Later, both from the So Far Gone mixtape and the unreleased track, Where Were You, which he co-produced with Boi-1da. As well as performing with Drake, Tennant has played keyboards for Keshia Chante, Glenn Lewis and has produced for such artists as Lil Wayne, Trey Songz, Jennifer Hudson and Bun B. He continues to act as musical director and play keyboard/piano while touring with Drake.

Davis Jake

Award winning music video and commercial director, Jake Davis is a graduate of New York University's Tisch School of the Arts and he directed the music video for the song Successful, from the mixtape So Far Gone. The song was co-written and featured the American R&B singer Trey Songz, and also featured on Songz's third album, Ready.

The Successful video, which was released on 31 August 2009, featured Drake's hometown of Toronto as the backdrop. The video went on to win the MuchVIBE Hip-Hop Video of the Year and the Cinematographer of the Year awards at the 2010 MuchMusic Video Awards ceremony, held on 20 June at MuchMusic's headquarters in Toronto. On the night of the show Drake gave a live performance of his single Over to thousands of fans on John Street, from an outdoor stage opposite the MuchMusic's HQ.

It is not the first time Davis has worked with Drake and Young Money artists. He directed the TV commercial for Lil Wayne's 2010 album, Rebirth, with Oliver El-Khatib again serving as Creative Director. Davis also produced a 30-second video test shot of Drake, which was premiered at the Apple store in New York's SoHo in December 2010, which was used as part of an advertising campaign for Drake's second album, Thank Me Later.

Davis has worked with a who's who of the music industry, embracing every genre and has created music videos, filmed live performances, and documentaries for artists including, My Chemical Romance, Flyleaf, Kanye West, 50 Cent, Nelly, Snoop Dogg, Korn, and OneRepublic.

Davis Jamil

Drake's tour manager, Jamil Davis has had a meteoric rise in the music business since he started his career as a local radio DJ and occasionally serving as a manager for local bands in his home town of Los Angeles. He got his big break after completing an internship with Universal Records, before taking on bigger and more popular artists as tour manager until eventually managing Lil Wayne on some of the biggest grossing tours ever. In 2010 he became the tour manager for Wayne's young protégé Drake. While on tour with Drake, Davis' duties vary on a day-to-day or even city-to-city basis. In general, he books hotel rooms for Drake's entourage and makes sure everything is satisfactory with the rooms and at each venue where the show is to take place.

He liaises closely with Drake's publicist in New York, Sarah Cunningham, and obtains a list of the accredited media outlets which will be invited to conduct interviews before each show, with about 30-minutes generally being allocated to the media.

Davis works closely with Drake's production manager and the pair will ensure that everything associated with loading all the equipment in and out at every venue, carrying out sound checks and transporting all the equipment to and from each city is conducted in a timely manner. Other duties include ensuring that all the back-stage rider demands are met for Drake and his entourage to relax with after the show. (see **Rider**) He will also ensure there are no problems with curfew restrictions, due to some cities having time restraints to limit noise disturbance to local residents from the music venues. Last but not least, a very important part of the role is to work closely with the promoter of the show and ensure that the percentages for performing are met and paid in full.

Dedication 3

Dedication 3 is a mixtape by DJ Drama and Lil Wayne and is the third in the Dedication series, following on from the highly successful Dedication 2. The mixtape introduced many of the artists recently signed to Young Money Entertainment, including Mack Maine, Gudda Gudda, Jae Millz, Lil Twist, Tyga, Nicki Minaj and Drake, who features on the track called Stuntin.

- Released: 14 November 2008
- Mixtape:
- Label: Young Money
- Length: 73:37
- Producer: DJ Drama, Various Others

Degrassi: The Next Generation

Aubrey Graham cemented his acting career by playing the role of Jimmy Brooks, a character on *Degrassi: The Next Generation*. He was accepted for the part after passing his first-ever audition when he was 14. His character, basketball player Jimmy Brook's first appearance was in Season 1: Episode 3 called *Family Politics* and aired on CTV on Sunday 4 November 2001.

Aubrey Graham played the character of Jimmy Brooks for eight years – which covered eight seasons of the show – who in Season 4 becomes paralysed from the waist down after being shot by his classmate Rick Murray. The episode in which he gets shot, *Time Stands Still* was one of the most-watched television shows in Canadian TV history. Graham's role on the show eventually ended in 2009 when his character graduated from Degrassi High School and moved to New York.

Aubrey Graham appeared in a total of 138 episodes; his first line in the show was to fellow character Ashley 'What was that all about?' He delivered his final line in Season 8: Episode 8, *Lost In Love Part 1*, to the character Spinner. Referring to Spinner and Jane he says: 'Just make sure that no matter what, you're going to be there for each other.'

Graham also played the Jimmy Brooks character in the 2008 television movie *Degrassi: Spring Break Movie.*

Drake the rapper is mentioned in the 2010 television movie *Degrassi Takes Manhattan,* making him only one of two Degrassi actors along with Shenae Grimes, who exist within the series' fictional universe independently of their characters.

Jimmy Brooks has rapped twice on the show; the first was during Season 3 while he was rehearsing for a Battle of The Band competition, he and his friend, Spinner, lay down a quick freestyle, but they were quickly discouraged from going any further by their friends due to being so bad. In Season 7 as part of a storyline regarding Ashley trying to return to music, Brooks lays down a rap verse to perform with Ashley. This time the flow was great and was surely a sign of things to come.

While he was playing Brooks on Degrassi, at home he was writing raps and rhymes and performing in the basement of his home, waiting for his opportunity to shine. He finally made the decision to release a mixtape of self-penned raps and verses using the money he made from the show and a loan from his uncle to fund its release. The mixtape was recorded and mixed in Toronto at the BCP Studios by B Joseph, titled Room for Improvement and released in 2006. To help promote the mixtape he would give away the music on the Degrassi set and at local clubs to gain maximum publicity, with his mother helping to post the tapes out to customers and friends.

The following year he released his second mixtape, Comeback Season, which resulted in some airplay in the US after the music video for Replacement Girl was featured on BET as 'New Joint of the Day.' The track also featured American singer-songwriter Trey Songz.

Aubrey Graham's role on the show finally came to an end in 2009 owing to the producers deciding to take the show in a different direction. Drake said at the time:

> 'When they pulled the plug on our generation of Degrassi, that was the moment my life changed. I called my agent and said 'look man I know you're getting me lots of auditions but I'm now gonna' concentrate on my music.'

.....and the rest as they say is history.

Degrassi: The Facts

Degrassi: The Next Generation, was the fourth fictional series in the Degrassi franchise and it succeeded *The Kids of Degrassi Street*, *Degrassi: Junior High* and *Degrassi: High*. Like its predecessors, the series follows a group of seven and eight grade students at Degrassi Community School who face various challenges of teenage life, such as poor self-image, peer pressure, child abuse, sexual identity, gang violence, self-harm, teenage pregnancy and drug use.

The series was created by Linda Schuyler and Yan Moore and produced by Epitome Pictures in association with CTV, with the first episode televised in September 1979.

The series is filmed at Epitome's studios in Toronto, Ontario, rather than on the real De Grassi Street, from which the franchise takes its name.

Degrassi: The Next Generation, premiered on Canadian TV on 14 October 2001 and received critical praise throughout its run from many different outlets including, *Entertainment Weekly*, *The New York Times* and AfterElton.com. In its initial years, the show was frequently the most watched domestic drama series in Canada.

At the conclusion of Season 12 in June 2013, a total of 317 episodes have aired.

The episode featuring the shooting of Drake's character Jimmy Brooks gave the series an all-time high audience of 930,000 Canadian viewers.

Season 13 premiered on 11 July 2013 on MuchMusic in Canada and TeenNick in the US, with the name shortened to Degrassi. The series is scheduled for 40 episodes.

The Degrassi franchise has won numerous awards, from the Geminis, Writers Guild of Canada and Directors Guild of Canada, with international honours from the Teen Choice Awards, Young Artists Awards and Prix Jeunesse.

The current executive producers are Schuyler, her husband Stephen Stohn and Brendon York.

The show was the highest-rated show on *TeenNick* in the United States. In 2004, one episode received just under a million viewers.

The theme music, Whatever It Takes was written by Austin Russell, Jody Colero and Stephen Stohn, with Colero and Stohn also writing the lyrics.

Linda Schyler, the series creator who spotted the potential in the 13 year old Aubrey Graham during auditions has said:

'We were looking for an athletic, friend of everybody type. Aubrey had a charm about him and warmth, that same beautiful smile he has now. He was green as anything, but willing to do whatever it takes.'

She added;

'We would do a string of mall tours south of the border when the series broke in the US and we would get 3-4,000 kids and Aubrey even then had this aura about him like a rock star.'

Degrassi: Unscripted

In 2005, Aubrey Graham took part in a series of mini documentaries for *TeenNick* called, *Degrassi: Unscripted*. His episode was one in a series of eight which followed some of the most popular stars of the show relaxing at home and showing their interests away from the cameras. The episodes aired from 27 August 2004 to 17 June 2005.

On his show, which aired on 10 June 2005, Graham is shown at his home, in the studio recording tracks for his mixtapes, and talking about working with record companies. He also talks about his character in the show, and how he played the role as a disabled person after his character, Jimmy Brooks, was shot and paralysed by a fellow student.

Digital GIrl

Digital Girl is a song performed by Jamie Foxx, featuring Drake, Kanye West and The Dream who also produced the song alongside Tricky Stewart. The song is the fourth track on Foxx's third studio album, Intuition. The music video for the track, directed by Hype Williams premiered on 20 August 2009, with Drake opening the video with his verses.

- Released: 6 July 2009
- Album: Intuition
- Label: J Records
- Length: 4:38
- Writers: Eric Bishop, Aubrey Graham. Kanye West, Terius Nash
- Producer: Tricky Stewart, The Dream
- Music Video: Hype Williams

Diploma

When he was 15 years old, Drake dropped out of Toronto's Forest Hill Collegiate Institute, walking out on a history lesson after the teacher told him 'if you walk out of this lesson, don't come back!' He didn't, and decided to put all his efforts into his music career.

Fast forward to 2012…after failing to complete his studies, he has always had an ambition to finally complete a diploma, especially as his mother is a retired school teacher. During the summer of 2012, instead of partying in VIP rooms, supping on expensive champagne or on the tour bus travelling to another gig, Drake finally achieved his dream by completing his diploma. He explained:

'I'm actually spending my summer graduating High School, that's my main focus after the OVO Festival on 5 August.'

Drake informed all his fans through Twitter that he had finally completed his diploma with high scores to boot. He commented '97 per cent on my final exam and 88 per cent in the course, it's one of the greatest feelings in my entire life.'

At Jarvis Collegiate Institute in Toronto, with his diploma in hand Drake shared life lessons with fellow students at his graduation night. He also acknowledged his mother and especially Uncle Steve who was in the audience for his guidance and support throughout his teenage years. Drake followed fellow Canadian Justin Bieber who graduated from St. Michael Catholic School in Stratford, Ontario after taking the courses electronically on the web while touring the world.

Discography

Since 2006, Drake has released three studio albums, one Extended Play and three mixtapes, from which he has released numerous singles. He has also appeared as the featured guest artist on over fifty songs with some of the biggest names in rap and hip-hop.

Owing to the phenomenal amount body of work Drake has produced since he hit the world stage in 2009, only a selection of his titles as the main artist have been identified below, many of which have been certified gold or platinum by the Recording Industry Association of America. His work, as featured artist on songs which have also been certified by the RIAA, are covered within the features section of the book in more detail. (see **Features**) The numbers required to be sold for certification are as follows:

- Gold: 500,000 sales
- Platinum: 1,000,000 sales (or x multiples)

Mixtapes

Title	Details
Room for Improvement	Released: February 14,2006 Label: All Things Fresh Formats: CD, digital download
Comeback Season	Released: 2007 Label: October's Very Own Formats: CD, digital download
So Far Gone	Released: February 13, 2009 Label: October's Very Own Formats: CD, digital download

Extended Play

Title	Certification	Details
So Far Gone	Gold	Released: 15 September 2009 Label: Young Money, Cash Money Universal Republic Formats: CD, digital download

Albums

Title	Certification	Details
Thank Me Later	x2 Platinum	Released: 15 June 2010 Label: Young Money, Cash Money, Universal Motown Formats: CD, LP, digital download
Take Care	x2 Platinum	Released: 15 November 2011 Label: Young Money Cash Money Universal Republic Formats: CD, LP, digital download
Nothing Was the Same	x2 Platinum	Released: 24 September 2013 Label: Young Money, Cash Money, Republic Formats: CD, LP, digital download

72

Singles Title	Certification	Details
Replacement Girl		Released: 2009 Mixtape: Comeback Season
Best I Ever Had	x2 Platinum	Released: 2009 Album: So Far Gone
Successful	Gold	Released: 2009 Album: So Far Gone
Forever		Released: 2009 Album: More Than A Game
I'm Going In	Platinum	Released: 2009 Album: So Far Gone
Over	Gold	Released: 2010 Album: Thank Me Later
Find Your Love	Platinum	Released: 2010 Album: Thank Me Later
Miss Me	Gold	Released: 2010 Album: Thank Me Later
Fancy		Released: 2010 Album: Thank Me Later
Headlines	Platinum	Released: 2011 Album: Take Care
Make Me Proud	Platinum	Released: 2011 Album: Take Care
The Motto	x3 Platinum	Released: 2011 Album: Take Care
Marvin's Room		Released: 2011 Album: Take Care
Take Care	x2 Platinum	Released: 2011 Album: Take Care
HYFR	Gold	Released: 2011 Album: Take Care
Crew Love		Released:2011 Album: Take Care
Started From the Bottom	x2 Platinum	Released: 2013 Album: Nothing Was the Same
Hold On, Were Going Home	Platinum	Released 2013 Album: Nothing Was the Same

DJ Future the Prince

Drake's friend and official DJ since 2007, Adel Prince Nur aka DJ Future the Prince, has certainly come a long way from his first and only job at the age of 15 in a local record store. Now he hosts Grammy after parties, MTV award shows and Super Bowl parties in Miami to private parties for Jay Z, LeBron James, Lil Wayne and Kanye West. Nur bought his first deck of old turntables when he was still a teenager, and with a handful of records started DJ'ing for family and friends to supplement his wages from the store. While he was working in the record store, he met and became friendly with all the top local DJs who would come in and buy records. Explaining how he obtained his stage name, he said:

> 'My middle name is Prince, so that's where the Prince part came from, and when I started DJ'ing the other DJs took me under their wing and allowed me to open up for them. So at a young age, a 16 year old kid in a club made everyone say like 'You're the guy, you're going to be the future, and the name just stuck.'

After meeting Tyrone 'T RexXx' Edwards, who was the Business Arts co-ordinator, Nur joined the Remix Project, which is an inner city charitable organisation based in Toronto. It was on a trip to Brazil with Remix and Schools Without Borders that Nur helped to build a recording studio working one-to-one with the locals inside the favelas of Rio de Janeiro, which he has called a great character-building trip.

Returning to Toronto, Nur started hanging out at the Avocado Supper Club where Drake and his band, The Renaissance where playing and the two were introduced by mutual friends. After running into each other continually over the following months in various clubs, and having a lot of mutual interests they eventually became close friends.

They also decided they liked the same types of music and Drake offered Prince the role of his DJ while touring. Nur is currently an ambassador for the Remix Project.

DJ Smallz

Jonathan Murray, aka DJ Smallz is an American hip-hop DJ, who was born in Japan while his father was stationed there with the US Navy. In 2006 he hosted Drake's first mixtape, Room for Improvement.

Known for his Southern Smoke street brand, which includes mixtapes and Southern Smoke Radio, Smallz is also famous for hosting CDs for relatively unknown artists. In the past his tapes have featured artists such as Young Buck, Ludacris, Master P, Lil Wayne and of course, Drake.

Smallz has been instrumental in giving many future stars their first break, as in 2007 when he hosted the first annual Southern Smoke College Tour with breaking artists Flo-Rida and Jamie Foxx headlining.

Drizzy

Verse three of the song Congratulations – the last track on Drake's 2009 mixtape, So Far Gone – helps explain how Drake acquired his nickname Drizzy. A lot of new fans thought Lil Wayne had given Drake the moniker Drizzy, when they heard him shout out the Canadian rapper at the 2008 MTV Video Music Awards, which honour the best music videos from the previous year, on 7 September at Paramount Pictures Studios in California. While Leona Lewis launched into the hook of Nina Simeone's, Please Don't Let Me Be Misunderstood, Wheezy rapped 'Drizzy Drake, I love you bwoy!' and with that Drake and everybody else watching the show knew he had arrived.

Lil Wayne first heard about Drake in early 2008 when he was given a mixtape of Drake's music from Rap-A-Lot founder James Prince's son, Jas Prince. After listening to just two tracks, he liked what he had heard and immediately called Drake, inviting him to fly to Houston and tour with him. After joining Wayne in Houston the duo recorded a couple of songs during this time, including Ransom, the original version of I Want This Forever and the remix to Drake's song Brand New.

Ransom also includes shout-outs to 'Drizzy Drake Rogers' and the misunderstanding occurred due to Drake's e-mail address being drizzydrake@rogers.com. Due to the pair corresponding through e-mail, Wayne thought Drake's real name must be Drizzy Drake Rogers – Rogers being the Canadian Internet Server – and he called him that on tracks and in interviews. In reality, Drake's father Dennis had chosen Drake for his middle name, and an original All Things Fresh member from Toronto, Footz gave him the nickname Drizzy in the early 2000s as mentioned on Congratulations.

Drought is Over (Friends with Money)

After releasing his So Far Gone mixtape in January, Drake quickly put out a new free mixtape for download on 14 May 2009 called Drought Is Over (Friends with Money). The mixtape was a compilation of his best material to date, with a few new songs and radio freestyles, with six featuring Lil Wayne and Trey Songz on a further three. The mixtape consisted of 24 tracks in total and included his two smash hits, Successful and Best I Ever Had.

Dual Nationality

Drake has dual nationality: Canadian through his mother and American through his father.

eBay

Drake was an eBay fanatic in his teenage days, often spending hours online buying and selling clothes, electronic goods and anything else which came to hand, much to the amusement of his friends. When he was 17 he bought a microphone for $200 off a guy from Virginia. The microphone had an autograph allegedly signed by one of his favourite hip-hop singers at that time, 'Pusha T' of the group Clipse. Although he could not prove the authenticity of the autograph, he fixed the mike up at the right height in his basement at home, constantly using it for imaginary celebrity interviews and singing sessions. He also used the microphone when he started singing with his band, The Renaissance, when they played at the Avocado Supper Club in Toronto.

Eventually, with the constant use of the microphone, the autograph inevitably started to fade and he finally parted with the microphone, not really knowing if the signature was indeed genuine.

Eccleston 'X' Adrian

Adrian 'X' Eccleston is a Canadian guitarist who is widely regarded as one of the best to come out of Toronto. His musical talents have led him to tour the world, working with artists such as Kylie Minogue, Nelly Furtado and more recently, Drake.

Before embarking upon his worldwide music career, Eccleston completed the Claude Watson program for the Arts at Earl Haig Secondary School in Toronto before continuing his studies as a jazz performer at the University of Toronto. Eccleston cites American legend Jimi Hendrix as a great musical influence and lists artists such as The Edge, Shuggie, Otis and Prince as his inspirations. His distinctive style and guitar playing skills have been described as ear-bending.

In March 2010, Eccleston joined Drake as guitarist and some time musical director and while on tour he can be found playing the guitar solos, using the Mesa/Boogie amplifiers he has used for the best part of a decade. He has also been credited with co-writing Cece's Interlude from the 2010 platinum-selling album Thank Me Later, the hit singles Headlines and Marvin's Room on Drake's follow up album, Take Care and Furthest Thing from Nothing Was the Same, released in 2013. With his stage presence, creative vibe and blazing guitar solos, Eccleston has become one of the most sought after live guitarists at present, and is a permanent feature of Drake's stage show.

Education

Drake attended a number of schools during his teenage years, due to the fact that his family regularly moved house because of their financial difficulties. Drake attended Forest Hill Elementary and Collegiate Institute and Vaughan Road Academy which are both situated in Toronto, Ontario. He also attended a Jewish day school when he was younger. He failed to complete his education and dropped out of high school when he was 15, going on to eventually complete his diploma in 2012.

Edwards 'T-RexXx' Tyrone

Already a well-established figure in the Toronto urban/hip-hop community, Tyrone 'T-RexXx' Edwards is now host of the newly revamped RAPCITY, following on from his idols and previous hosts, Master T, Michael Williams and Traci Melchor. Drake was interviewed on New Year's Day 2011 for the inaugural show which was due to be aired 12 days later, with the interview pre-recorded as Drake was due to embark on his tour of the UK that evening. Tyrone had established his reputation as Canada's party animal by throwing BBQs and birthday parties in Toronto, eventually graduating to producing and hosting events for some of the biggest names in hip-hop, Jay Z and Drake.

On 31 October 2009, Edwards attended the Air Canada Center to see Drake join Jay Z on stage in Toronto, to sing Successful. After the show Edwards, the self styled 'party animal' who organises Drake's Toronto parties when he's in town, joined Drake, Jay Z and a small group of friends at a Queens Street bar for the after-party. Edwards said of the night:

> 'The budget has changed but the vibe hasn't changed. No paparazzi or hangers on, just a select circle of good friends, looking for a good time and then we watched Jay Z take a turn mixing cocktails, it was a great Halloween night.'

Edwards is actively involved in the local community and takes great pride as a mentor and coach for the underprivileged youth of Toronto. He is the founder of Concrete Hoops, a not-for-profit basketball camp that teaches life skills incorporated with the love of the game. He is also a Business Arts Program Leader in the Toronto based youth-oriented Remix Project. (see **Remix Project**)

F

Father

Drake's father, Dennis Graham hails from the Whitehaven area of Memphis, Tennessee. Of African-American ancestry, Graham played drums for the legendary Jerry Lee Lewis, and it's fair to say the Graham family bloodline has music deep in its soul. Dennis' brother is Larry Graham, a bassist best known for his work in the funk band Sly and the Family Stone, and as the front man/founder of Graham Central Station. Then there is Mabon 'Teenie' Hodges, another of Drake's uncles who is best known for co-writing some of American soul singer Al Green's hits including, Take Me To The River and Love and Happiness.

After divorcing his wife Sandi Graham, when Aubrey was just 5 years old, Dennis regularly travelled to Toronto, returning to Memphis with Aubrey, so that they could spend the summer vacation together. Trips to Memphis and the time spent with his father – listening to the music in the car on the 22 hour trip and seeing him working in the recording studio – influenced the young Aubrey in his future career and is the reason he became so good at his flow and verses, according to his father. The soulful, rhythmic style associated with Drake, has often been attributed to his father and the black music scene synonymous with Memphis. The young Aubrey would often sit on his father's lap in the recording studio while his father played piano and sang. He also had lessons on the piano as a small boy, as well as accompanying his father on his late-night club gigs.

'That's why his metaphors are so phenomenal now, because he's been in Memphis!' said his father in an interview after the album Take Care hit the charts.

Dennis Graham taught his son to sing the classic Lou Reed song Ride Sally Ride, which he used to perform on stage as part of his set. During the performance he would often bring the young Aubrey on stage, letting him develop his early musical talent in front of a live audience. Unfortunately, the relationship Dennis Graham has had with his son throughout his life has been mixed. Drake has described his father as being the anti role-model when compared to the relationship he has had with his mother Sandi.

Drake has said of their early relationship: 'I'll never be disappointed again, because I don't expect anything from him anymore.' He went on, 'There were too many times when he let me down, looking through the window waiting for a car that never came.'

Recently, Drake's relationship with his father has improved, with Dennis regularly seen in the audience at Drake's shows, and the pair being photographed together in restaurants and nightclubs, he also accompanied Drake to the Grammy Awards ceremony in 2012. Drake has not ruled out a duet with his father on an upcoming album, to follow on from his father's cameo role on Drake's hit single Successful. In 2013, Dennis appeared in the music video for Worst Behavior, a single off the Nothing Was the Same album. The video set in Memphis, Tennessee where Drake spent his summer vacations, features many familiar locations to him including his grandmother's house and his father's old recording studio.

Favourites

Drake's favourite basketball, hockey team, movie stars and restaurants are set out below.

Basketball: Drake has been photographed at numerous basketball games, but he has three favourite teams; the Kentucky Wildcats College team (see **Basketball**) and the Miami Heat, due to his close friendship with star player LeBron James who hosted the So Far Gone mixtape promotion night in 2009. He is also a season-ticket holder for the Toronto Raptors and again attends games as often as his busy schedule allows. In 2013, Drake was appointed Global Ambassador for the Raptors, with a brief to widen and enhance the brand.

Hockey Team: the Toronto Maple Leafs, a professional ice hockey franchise based in Toronto. They are members of the Northeast Division of the Eastern Conference of the National Hockey League, and have won the famous Stanley cup thirteen times, the last time was in 1967.

Movie Stars: African-American stars Sidney Poitier, Denzil Washington and Will Smith. Interestingly in the documentary Degrassi Unscripted, Drake revealed that a fan had written to him and predicted he would make up the trio of famous African-American male actors after Poitier and Washington.

Restaurant: Vivoli, an Italian restaurant situated on College Street in the heart of Little Italy, Toronto. The restaurant is also mentioned on the sleeve credits on his Take Care album. Drake calls the restaurant his escape when the world goes crazy.

Features

Drake had appeared as the named featured artist on numerous tracks, with most of today's major rap and hip-hop stars, since he first featured on Change You with Jenna G in 2006. Because there are so many features, we have decided to list those which have been certified gold or platinum by the Recording Industry Association of America.

All have been covered individually in more detail within the book and they are listed in chronological order below.

Hit singles with Drake as Featured Artist

Title	Main Artist	Album	Certified
Money To Blow	Birdman	Priceless	Platinum
Right Above It	Lil Wayne	I Am Not A Human Being	2xPlatinum
Aston Martin Music	Rick Ross	Teflon Don	Gold
What's My Name?	Rihanna	Loud	3xPlatinum
Moment 4 Life	Nicki Minaj	Pink Friday	Platinum
I'm On One	DJ Khaled	We The Best Forever	3xPlatinum
She Will	Lil Wayne	Tha Carter 1V	3xPlatinum
No Lie	2 Chainz	Based on a TRU Story	Platinum
Pop That	French Montana	Excuse My French	Platinum
F* Problems	ASAP Rocky	Long Live ASAP	Platinum
Poetic Justice	Kendrick Lamar	Good Kid M.A.A.D City	Gold
Love Me	Lil Wayne	I Am Not A Human Being 2	Platinum
No New Friends	DJ Khaled	Suffering from Success	Gold

Find Your Love

Find Your Love, was the second and most successful single from Drake's debut album, Thank Me Later.

Produced and written by Kanye West, the song is unique as it features Drake almost exclusively singing and it has been favourably compared to West's 808s and Heartbreak. Released on 5 May 2010, the single reached number five on the US Billboard Hot 100, and number three on the US Hot R&B/Hip-Hop Song chart. It was certified platinum by the Recording Industry Association of America with sales of over 1 million copies.

The music video directed by Anthony Mandler, was filmed in Jamaica and met with some controversy from the Jamaican Tourism Industry, owing to their fear that the video was confirming the stereotype of the Island's gun and gangster culture, because of the content of the video and the use of alleged local gangsters as extras.

- Released: May 5 2010
- Album: Thank Me Later
- Label: Young Money, Cash Money, Universal Motown
- Length: 3:29
- Writers: Aubrey Graham, Kanye West, Jeff Bhasker, Patrick Reynolds
- Producer: Kanye West, Jeff Bhasker, No1.D
- Music Video: Anthony Mandler

Fiona Melanie

Melanie Fiona is a Canadian-born R&B and soul recording artist. Her debut album, The Bridge released in 2009 on the Universal Motown label, included the hit single, It Kills Me which topped the Billboard Hot R&B/Hip-Hop Song chart. The song also earned her the first of five Grammy Nominations for Best Female R&B Vocal Performance. In 2012 she finally won two Grammy Awards for her collaboration with Cee Lo Green on the song, Fool for You which won Best Traditional R&B Performance and Best R&B Song at the 53rd Awards, held at the Staples Center, Los Angeles.

Fiona has also won a Juno award – which is awarded annually to acknowledge Canadian artists and bands – for R&B/Soul Recording of The Year with her track, Gone and Never Coming Back. She has known Drake since they performed together in his first band The Renaissance in 2005. In the band Fiona sang duets with Aion 'Voyce' Clarke, while Drake was MC for the evening, singing harmonies and rapping verses to the diners at the Avocado Club in Toronto, where they had a residency. After the band split up Fiona took up various roles as a solo artist and as part of the Canadian girl trio XQuisite, with Andreena Mills and Nicole Holness.

In 2007 Fiona travelled to the USA with her executive producer Carmen Murray of Title 9 Productions, where her career really started to take shape. Her first break came when her song, Somebody Come Get Me appeared on the 2008 Reggae Gold Compilation album under her stage name of Syren Hall. At that stage in her career her musical influences were mainly Caribbean, inspired by her family heritage. After receiving positive reviews, she was invited to support Kanye West on his 2008 Glow in the Dark European Tour. The tour went on to become the third highest earning tour of the year, grossing $30 million from the 49 concerts.

Fiona sang the Canadian National Anthem on Sunday 20 February 2011, at the NBA All Star Entertainment Series weekend in Los Angeles, where she was reunited with the other original members of The Renaissance. Drake attended with Rihanna to perform their smash hit, What's My Name? during the half-time show. (see **Renaissance The**)

Her second album, The MF Life, released in 2012, included a Drake song called, I Been That Girl and the pair continue to collaborate together. Fiona is an ambassador for The Remix Center in Toronto.

Firsts

Details of Drake's first car, headliner tour, magazine cover, music video, OVO artist signed, radio airplay, rap album he listened to and solo performance in the US are listed below.

Car: a black Accura TSX.

Headliner Tour: in preparation for his debut album, Thank Me Later, Drake embarked on his first North American tour – the Away From Home tour – which started on 5 April, 2010 at Slippery Rock University.

Magazine Cover: in September 2009, Drake featured on the cover of the Fader Magazine.

Music Video: in 2006, Drake featured on the single, Change You with R&B singer-songwriter and fellow Canadian Jenna G. In February 2007 he appeared in his first music video for the single, which was directed by Chris G. The video was released just prior to the release of his own music video for Replacement Girl, featuring Trey Songz from his Comeback Season mixtape. Change You, produced by Dre Knight, went on to have heavy rotation play on Flow 93.5FM and other major Canadian radio stations.

OVO Artist: PartyNextDoor is a Canadian singer/rapper who is the first artist to be signed to Drake's OVO Label. His first mixtape, the self-titled PartyNextDoor was released onto Drake's OVO Sound Cloud in April 2013.

Radio Airplay: the first of Drake's records to receive air play on the radio was City Is Mine, the seventh track from Drake's first mixtape Room For Improvement, which was released in 2006. The track was produced by Boi-1da.

Rap Album: the first rap album Drake listened to was Snoop Dogg's 1993 quadruple platinum selling debut album Doggystyle but due to the explicit content of the songs, his mother would not let him play the music in the house. The only way he could listen to the tape was while travelling with his father on the long drive down to Memphis, where Drake spent the summer holidays with his father's family after his parents' divorce.

Solo Performance (US): Drake played his first solo US performance at the Southern Illinois University Carbondale on 21 March 2009, in front of a sold-out crowd of 2,500.

Forest Hill Collegiate Institute

Forest Hill Collegiate Institute was founded in 1946, and is a public high school located in the wealthy predominately Jewish neighbourhood of Forest Hill, Toronto for grades 9-12. It was while attending Forest Hill that Drake began his acting career. One of his classmates introduced him to his father who was a casting agent in the entertainment industry. After a brief audition he was taken onto the talent agency's books and shortly afterwards landed his role as Jimmy Brooks on *Degrassi: The Next Generation*.

Drake attended Forest Hill Collegiate Institute, before moving on to Vaughan Academy, again in Toronto from where he dropped out to concentrate on his music career.

Forever

Originally recorded by Kardinal Offishall as Bring It Back, the beat was sold to Drake and he released it in the summer of 2008 as I Want This Forever, featuring Lil Wayne and Nut Da Kid.

The song was originally meant to be Drake's coming out single, but was leaked prior to the official release onto the internet.

Resurrected the following year and renamed Forever, the initial intention was for the song to have just Drake and Kanye West on the track, but it developed into a huge hip-hop monster collaboration, when Lil Wayne and Eminem joined the project. Leaking again on 26 August 2009, the release caused a frenzy among hip-hop fans, with Drake writing the hook and his verse and West penning his verse in response to Drake's. The song was produced by Boi-1da.

- Released: 27 August 2009
- Album: More Than A Game
- Label: Zone 4, Interscope, Shady, Aftermath
- Length: 5:58
- Writers: Aubrey Graham, Dwayne Carter Jr,Kanye West, Marshall Mathers, Matthew Samuels
- Producer: Matthew Samuels
- Music Video: Hype Williams

Drake performed the song live at the 52nd Grammy Award ceremony in 2010, with Wayne, Eminem and Travie Barker. Forever was also released as a single from the soundtrack to the LeBron James documentary *More Than A Game* and featured on Eminem's Relapse album. The song peaked at number one on the US Billboard Rap Song and number two on the Billboard Hot R&B/Hip-Hop song charts and was certified platinum with sales of over 1 million copies by the Recording Industry Association of America.

The music video, directed by Hype Williams was shot in Miami in September 2009 and featured cameo appearances from Birdman and LeBron James. Throughout the video there are photographs and clips of James playing basketball.

Fort York Boulevard

Apartment 1503 Fort York Boulevard, in downtown Toronto is the apartment where Noah Shebib and Drake laid down most of the tracks on the So Far Gone mixtape.

Foxx Jamie

Jamie Foxx is an American, two-time Grammy Award winning actor, comedian, musician and singer-songwriter who Drake has worked with on a number of occasions. He featured and co-wrote Digital Girl, a single from Foxx's 2009 album Intuition and featured again on Fall for Your Type, the third single from Foxx's fourth album, Best Night of My Life. Released in 2010, the track reached number one on the US Billboard Hot R&B/Hip-Hop Song chart. Fall for Your Type was originally meant to appear on Drake's Thank Me Later album but he decided against including the track on his album.

Multi talented Foxx has worked with some of the biggest names in the music industry, winning his first Grammy Award with Kanye West with Gold Digger. He has also won an Academy Award for Best Actor for his portrayal of blind pianist, Ray Charles in the 2004 biopic Ray.

- Released:12 November 2010
- Album: Best Night of My Life
- Label: J Records
- Length: 4:31
- Writers: Noah Shebib, Aubrey Graham, Noel Campbell
- Producer: Noah Shebib, Rico Love
- Music Video: Christopher Robinson

Francis and the Lights

Francis and the Lights are a New York synth-pop band who accompanied Drake on his first headlining tour of North American college campuses from April-June 2010. The Lights were personally chosen by Drake to join him on the road as his supporting act, along with fellow Canadian rapper k-os. The Lights front-man, Francis Farewell Starlite, also co-wrote and produced the second track Karaoke, from Drake's album, Thank Me Later.

While they were on the Away From Home tour, Drake asked Starlite if he had any music available and if so, to send it through to him and '40'. After sending through a number of beats and hearing nothing back, he then sent them a song he had been working on for a while. He had an immediate reaction with Drake saying he loved it and asking if he could use the song for his upcoming album Thank Me Later. That song was Karaoke, with Starlite saying that Drake didn't change the music much, but he has admitted that Drake's vocal had made the song more personal and ultimately better.

> 'He made it better, unquestionably from what I had... He made it very personal, but making some very subtle changes and doing his thing on it, obviously with the verses. He actually made it make sense in a way that it didn't make sense to me before.'

Francis and the Lights played at the first OVO festival on Sunday 1 August 2010 at the 17,000 seat Molson Amphitheatre in Toronto.

F***** Problems

F***** Problems is the second single off A$AP Rocky's debut album Long. Live. ASAP. The single, released on 24 October 2012, featured 2 Chainz, Kendrick Lamar and Drake.

The song reached number eight on the Billboard Hot 100, making it 2 Chainz, A$AP and Kendrick Lamar's most successful single to date, and was certified platinum by the Recording Industry Association of America with sales of over 1 million copies. The track was also significant because Drake co-produced the single alongside Noah '40' Shebib with him credited as C Papi, a shortened version of his instagram tag champagnepapi.

- Released: 24 October 2012
- Album: Long. Live. ASAP
- Label: Polo Grounds, RCA
- Length: 3:57
- Writers: Kendrick Lamar Duckworth, Rakim Mayers Noah Shebib, Aubrey Graham, Tauheed Epps, Sean Garrett
- Producers: Noah Shebib, C Papi
- Music Video: Sam Lecce, Clarke Jackson

G

Gawne Jenna

Drake worked with Canadian R&B singer/song-writer, Jenna Gawne, aka Jenna G on her 2006 single, Change You. The following year he appeared in the music video for the song, which was his first appearance in a major music video.

Gee Shawn

President of Music and Entertainment at SEFG, LLC and Head of Touring for the Blueprint Group, Shawn Gee has been Drake's business manager since 2009. He has been involved in the entertainment business since 1996, beginning with his first client, the Grammy Award winning hip-hop American band The Roots. Gee, who initially worked in finance on Wall Street, formed a relationship with Gee Roberson, from Hip Hop Since1978 through his management of Kanye West from 2005-10. During that time he helped develop West from a club and college act to the global superstar he is now, including overseeing his successful Glow in The Dark Tour. Maybe it was this track record which influenced Wayne and Roberson to leave their Young Money Entertainment artists under Gee's wing in the early days of their careers. Gee is also the tour manager for Nicki Minaj, J Cole and has managed Drake's successful Away from Home and Light Dreams and Nightmares tours.

Working with Lil Wayne since 2008, Gee has worked as tour manager for Wayne's last three tours, including the lucrative $47 million record-grossing 2009 I Am Still Music tour. All three tours were promoted by Al Haymon at Live Nation.

Gibbs Robert

Robert Gibbs works for International Creative Management and was responsible for domestic bookings for Drake's tours and shows until December 2011, when Drake moved to William Morris Endeavor Agency. (see **International Creative Management**)

Gibson CJ

CJ Gibson has been Drake's official road manager since Drake signed his record deal, but has been with him since the Away From Home tour. Gibson, who attended Jackson State University alongside his close friend Cortez Bryant and Lil Wayne, has appeared as a store clerk in Rihanna's music video, What's My Name featuring Drake. Drake has also mentioned Gibson in the songs, Miss Me and on Birdman's 4 My Town.

The pair have built up a close relationship since their time on the road and Drake hosted a party on 7 May 2011, at the Martini Room, in his home town of Jackson to celebrate Gibson's 23rd birthday. Drake even performed the new hot dance craze to 'Mo Head Swagg' by Jackson's Lil Al to the amusement of the watching party-goers.

In 2012 Gibson arranged for Drake to appear on the MTV show *Punk'd*. In the show Drake was unaware he was being filmed and was under the impression he was travelling to a meeting with the Vice President of the United States. Accompanied by Gibson and escorted by fake secret security guards, during the journey the pair encounter an earthquake, a heavily pregnant lady apparently going into labour and a run in with a fake taser gun, with Drake looking on shocked. Afterwards he tweeted presenter Ashton Kutcher saying he would remember that day forever.

Goapele

Goapele Mohlabane is an American Soul and R&B singer-songwriter. Drake covered her hit single Closer, from Goapele's second album Even Closer, on his mixtape Comeback Season. On the mixtape, Drake had used the original chorus – aided by fellow Canadian Andreena Mills as the female voice – with him rapping his verses over the original backing instrumental. The duo performed the song for the first time in public at the Warfield Theatre on 13 May 2010, when Goapele joined Drake on stage.

Recording since 2001, Goapele has released four studio albums, and her songs often cover human rights and social awareness issues. She has performed at rallies and various political events around the world and has been recognised for her human rights and social conscious work.

Gotti Yo

Yo Gotti is an American rapper from Memphis, Tennessee whom Drake pays homage to on his track, Under Ground Kings, from the album Take Care. Drake remembers watching Gotti recording in the studio in Memphis, while he was staying with his father and gives him a lot of credit for the way the experience of being in the studio watching and learning from him has helped to shape his early career.

Gotti has continued to release independent mixtapes and albums, since he released From Da Dope Game 2 Da Rap Game in 2000. Most of his mixtapes have been called the Cocaine Muziks and there have been seven in the series, the latest being released in 2012. He first came to prominence with the release of his 2003 independent album, Life which really elevated him to the higher ranks of Memphis rappers and brought him to the attention of a wider audience.

Gotti's first major label studio album, Live from the Kitchen, was released in 2012 on the RCA Records Label.

Graham 'Royalty' Christopher

Drake's cousin Christopher 'Royalty' Graham opened the show for him on 5 June 2012, at the FedEx Forum on the Memphis leg of his Club Paradise tour, with all the extended Graham family in attendance. Memphis rapper Royalty, who has been writing songs since 2004, released his first video L.O.V.E. featuring Drake's father Dennis on 4 November 2011. The video which was released onto Drake's OVO blog shows Dennis rapping a short verse to the camera along with Royalty. In 2012, Royalty released his first mixtape, From Victory to Kingdom.

Grammy Award

Grammy Awards are awarded annually by the National Academy of Recording Arts and Sciences. Drake has been nominated 13 times in his career, both as an individual songwriter/rapper and as a collaborator. Drake has performed at two Grammy shows, the first on 31 January 2010 at the Staples Center, Los Angeles when he was introduced onto the stage by movie director Quentin Tarantino. He performed alongside Lil Wayne and Eminem on their hit Forever, while Wayne and Eminem performed Drop The World from Wayne's album, Rebirth during the melody. Drake also performed at the 2011 Grammy Award show with Rihanna for the live debut performance of their smash hit, What's My Name?

Drake appeared at the 2012 Award ceremony as a presenter to introduce fellow Young Money artist Nicki Minaj onto the stage to perform her single, Roman Holiday. Drake has been accompanied to the show by his mother in 2011 and 2012.

He often jokes that it is the only way his mother gets to see him as he is always so busy. (see **Photographs**)

Drake finally won his first Grammy Award in 2013 for Best Rap Album, with Take Care. Accompanied by his Uncle Steve, Drake was interviewed on the red carpet and explained how he first heard about the news of his win. He said he was traveling to the ceremony by car listening to the stream on his iPad and when they heard the news his crew went crazy, got out of the car and started hugging each other, blocking the road. He then realized in the excitement that he had torn his jacket, so he called his tailor to meet him in a local hotel to do some urgent repairs.

Drake's Grammy Award Nominations

Year	Nominated Work	Award	Result
2010	Best I Ever Had	Best Rap Song	Nominated
2010	Best I Ever Had	Best Rap Performance	Nominated
2011	Drake	Best New Artist	Nominated
2011	Over	Best Rap Solo Performance	Nominated
2011	Fancy	Best Rap Performance	Nominated
2011	Thank Me Later	Best Rap Album	Nominated
2012	Moment 4 Life	Best Rap Performance	Nominated
2012	I'm On One	Best Rap Collaboration	Nominated
2012	What's My Name?	Best Rap Collaboration	Nominated
2013	HYFR	Best Rap Performance	Nominated
2013	The Motto	Best Rap Song	Nominated
2013	Take Care	Best Rap Album	**WON**

Green Gil

Gil Green is a film and music video director from Miami, Florida who started out as a DJ in the underground hip-hop scene selling mixtapes by day and hosting warehouse parties at night. Now he is one of the most-in-demand directors of both music video and commercials, and has worked with artists from many different genres including hip-hop, R&B, dancehall, pop, and latino. His first video for a major label was for the Slip N Slide/Atlantic label with Tricky Daddy, for his song America, in 2002. A huge Miami Heat basketball fan, he has also been involved in directing the team video for the past few years including the 2013 player introduction.

Gil Green has worked with many top artists during his career including Drake, Rick Ross, Lil Wayne, Beyonce, Nicki Minaj, Trey Songz and Usher, winning the BET Video Music Award for the Best Hip-Hop Video with Wayne's Lollipop. Since their first collaboration in 2009 with Birdman's 4 My Town – which also featured Lil Wayne – he has directed six music videos that have featured Drake.

Gil Green's Music Videos featuring Drake

Year	Artist	Single	Featuring
2009	Birdman	4 My Town	Drake, Lil Wayne
2009	DJ Khaled	Fed Up	Drake, Rick Ross, Usher, Young Jeezy
2009	Birdman	Money To Blow	Drake, Lil Wayne
2010	Diddy-Dirty Money	Loving You No More	Drake
2010	Rick Ross	Aston Martin Music	Drake
2011	DJ Khaled	I'm On One	Drake, Rick Ross

H

Haymon Al

Al Haymon is a promoter at Live Nation Entertainment who works closely with Shawn Gee, Drake's business manager when organising future tours. Live Nation/Haymon Ventures has promoted all of Lil Wayne's and Drake's tours to date.

Headlines

Headlines is the first single from Drake's second studio album, Take Care and was certified platinum by the American Recording Industry Association of America with sales of over 1 million copies.

- Released: 9 August 2011
- Album: Take Care
- Label: Young Money, Cash Money, Universal Republic
- Length: 3:56
- Writers: Noah Shebib, Adrian Eccleston, Aubrey Graham,
- Producer: Matthew Samuels, Noah Shebib,
- Music Video: Lamar Taylor & Hyghly Alleyne

Drake has said that the single provided the perfect tune to launch the album. He said of the single:

'I think it's great, the purpose of the record was to solely deliver a message. I could've gone with a radio friendly track, but I wanted to talk to people with this first record.'

Co-produced by Boi-1da and '40', Headlines was mixed at the Metalworks Studios, Missisauga, Ontario and was performed live for the first time at the Coliseum, in Windsor, Ontario on 4 August 2011. The song reached number two on the Billboard US Hot R&B/Hip-Hop Song and number one on the Billboard Rap Song charts, Drake's 10th record to hit the summit.

The music video for the song was directed by Lamar Taylor and Hyghly Alleyne, and was shot in and around Toronto. The video showcased a number of famous Toronto landmarks including showing Drake riding in the high-speed outside elevator up the CN Tower and on the pitch at the Rogers Center – formally the SkyDome – with the roof closing with a time-lapse ending, while the stadium's scoreboard is lit up in the background showing the album's title 'Take Care'.

Height

Drake is 6' 2" tall or 1m 68cm.

High School

Aubrey Graham attended Forest Hill Collegiate Institute, the first of two high schools he would attend. He also briefly attended Vaughan Road Academy which he later described as not by any means an easy school to attend, as it was located in a rough part of town. Graham dropped out of high school because he and his history teacher did not see eye to eye and eventually the tension came to a head during one lesson. Drake remembers:

> 'At the start of the lesson something just hit me that I didn't need to be there and it wasn't going to help my life. I wasn't getting a regular job or going to university, so I started packing my bags.'

On seeing him packing his bags, the teacher stopped him and said: 'If you do this make sure you never come back.' So he walked out and never returned.

That was the end of Graham's schooling; he had dropped out of high school. Later that evening, Aubrey was apprehensive about telling his mother – a former teacher – what he had done, as she had always instilled in him the importance of a good education. Fortunately, he was able to convince her it was for the best and she accepted his decision to quit school. It was his mother's support at this time which gave him the freedom to establish himself as an artist, and made him more determined to complete his diploma at a later stage in order to repay her. Despite dropping out of high school he later resumed his studies and finally graduated in 2012.

Hip Hop Since 1978

Hip Hop Since 1978 (HHS78) is a New York based management and production company founded by Gee Roberson and Kyambo 'Hip-Hop' Joshua in 2004. The two had previously been Directors of A&R for the entire Roc-A-Fella roster of artists. The first official project for HHS78 was Kanye West's debut album, The College Dropout which they executive co-produced. The album was certified double platinum with over 2 million sales and won a Grammy Award for Best Rap Album.

In 2009, HHS78 joined forces with Bryant Management and were involved in Drake's lucrative record deal with Universal Music. They also manage Lil Wayne's career with Roberson and Cortez Bryant executive co-producing Lil Wayne's album Tha Carter 3. Along with Wayne and Kanye West they continue to guide the careers of Drake, Noah '40' Shebib and Nicki Minaj.

With Bryant Management, HHS78 have gone on to form the brand development company The Blueprint Group, whose aim is to develop and expand their artist's marketability in all areas including touring, branding, film and television.

Hockey

Aubrey Graham played hockey for the Weston Red Wings and was a talented right winger due to his speed and guile, even making it to the Upper Canada College Hockey Camp, due to his early potential. Playing for a number of seasons, he eventually gave up the game on his mother's advice after he narrowly avoided sustaining a severe head injury during one game. He continues to attend games when his schedule allows and is a big fan of the Toronto Maple Leafs Ice Hockey team.

Hold On, We're Going Home

Produced by Canadian duo Majid Jordan – who are signed to Drake's record label OVO Sound – Noah '40' Shebib and Nineteen85, Hold On We're Going Home is the second single released from Drake's third studio album, Nothing Was the Same. Drake has said of the song that he hoped in 10 years time the song would be regularly played at wedding ceremonies and by people living away and reminiscing about home.

- Released: 7 August 2013
- Album: Nothing Was the Same
- Label: Young Money, Cash Money, Republic
- Length: 3:47
- Writers: Noah Shebib, Aubrey Graham,Majid Al Maskati, Jordan Ullman
- Producer: Noah Shebib, Majid Jordan, Nineteen85
- Music Video: Bill Pope

The single, certified platinum in October 2013 with sales of over 1 million copies, reached number one on the US Billboard Hot R&B/Hip-Hop Song chart and number four on the UK Singles chart, Drake's highest position to date in the UK. It also helped Drake score his 33rd top ten hit on the Billboard Hot R&B/Hip-Hop Song chart, putting him second to Lil Wayne who has amassed 36 top ten hits to date on the chart.

The music video for the single, directed by Bill Pope – who directed the Matrix and Superman films – has a setting in 1985 Miami and sees Drake attempting a daring rescue for his girl who has been kidnapped by a rival gang. During the video, Drake and his crew travel to rescue her from the rival stronghold, donning balaclavas and carrying plenty of firepower. The finale sees lots of shooting and explosions, with Drake eventually returning triumphantly, carrying his girl to freedom.

Hurtado Nikko

The renowned tattoo artist Nikko Hurtado, working out of his Black Anchor Collective in Hesperia, California is known for his realism and amazing coloured portraiture tattoos. Born in 1981, he displayed his artistic skills from an early age, drawing characters from comics and TV cartoon shows and copying his father and grandfather who were also gifted artists. After attending art class and learning to draw professionally at The Art Center of Pasadena, he started tattooing for a living in 2002. Constantly in demand, Hurtado travels the world attending conventions and producing amazing tattoos for his celebrity clientele and he has tattooed Drake on a number of occasions, including his '416' tribute to Aaliyah and Toronto and the portraits of Drake's recently deceased Uncle and Grandmother. (see **Tattoos**)

Hush 'Young Tony'

The Toronto rapper and homie of Drake has been on the scene since the early 2000s. Growing up in Scarborough, Ontario, he eventually moved to the east end neighborhood of Parma Court in North York, which has built up a reputation for developing top underground rappers and hip-hop artists. Under his rap name 'Young Tony' he fronted a three-man rap band called Deep Pockets and established his name with the 2006 release of the mixtapes, Talk Of Da Town Vol 1-2, a series of freestyles and tales from the hood.

Recently he has been working with Boi-1da on a number of new features and is a close member of Drake's OVO crew. Drake has said that he loves feed-back especially if it is from Hush – who is usually there for every performance – due to his own experiences in hip-hop and rap. Drake paid him a warm tribute on the album sleeve credits of his debut studio album, Thank Me Later.

HYFR

The song HYFR is the fifth single taken from Drake's second studio album, Take Care and features Lil Wayne. While listening to a number of tracks from DJ Screw's mixtape in the studio, Drake liked a song from Houston rapper Cedric Hill, better known as E.S.G. called Swangin' and Bangin' which gave him the concept for HYFR. After fellow Torontonian and producer Tyler 'T-Minus' Williams worked the beats, Drake completed the vocals.

The single was certified gold by the Recording Industry Association of America, selling over 500,000 copies and was nominated for the Best Rap Performance at the 2013 Grammy Awards, eventually losing out to Jay Z and Kanye West for their performance with smash hit N***** in Paris.

- Released: 24 April 2012
- Album: Take Care
- Label: Young Money, Cash Money, Universal Republic
- Length: 3:27
- Writers: Aubrey Graham, Dwayne Carter Jr, Cedric Hill, Anthony Palaman, K Samir, Noah Shebib, Tyler Williams
- Producer: T Minus
- Music Video: Director X

The music video, filmed inside Miami's Temple Israel is a tribute to Drake's Jewish heritage and shows him at a Bar Mitzvah ceremony with Trey Songz, Lil Wayne, Mack Maine and Noah Shebib, amongst others making cameo appearances. Directed by Director X (see **X Director**) the video won the Best Hip-Hop Video at the 2012 MTV Video Music Awards.

I

I Am Still Music Tour

The I Am Still Music Tour commenced just 6 months after Lil Wayne's release from prison on a weapon possession charge, for which he served 8 months of the year-long sentence. The tour, which started on the 16 March 2011 in Providence, Rhode Island, eventually finished 67 shows later on the 11 September 2011, in Woodlands, Texas.

Having previously joined Wayne on his I Am Music Tour in 2008-9, Drake was due to be on the follow-up tour alongside fellow Young Money artist Nicki Minaj and Rick Ross. Rumours had circulated that Drake had dropped out of the tour due to a misunderstanding about alleged unpaid royalties, but Drake explained prior to the tour that he had been touring since March and that he needed to take time out to work on his new album. He went on to tell his fans they can expect him to make surprise appearances during the tour. He did eventually perform during the tour in Washington, DC, Dallas, Houston, Miami, Florida and his home town Toronto gig on 19 August 2011, appearing with Wayne, Drake performed Miss Me and Forever.

Walking onto the stage in Washington, DC, he tried to dispel rumours of a split with the Young Money camp. Explaining to the sold-out audience, Drake stated that prior to the show Wayne had looked him in the eyes and asked if he wanted out of Young Money, and he had looked right back into Wayne's eyes saying he wanted this thing forever, before beginning his set to rousing applause from the crowd. The tour was produced by Live Nation and Al Haymon Ventures and grossed $47 million from the North American leg alone.

I'm Goin' In

I'm Goin' In, was released on 27 October 2009, and is the third and final single released from Drake's So Far Gone EP. The song featured Young Money associates Lil Wayne and Young Jeezy and was certified platinum by the Recording Industry Association of America with over 1 million sales.

- Released: 27 October 2009
- Album: So Far Gone
- Label: Young Money, Cash Money, Universal Motown
- Length: 3:45
- Writers: Aubrey Graham, Dwayne Carter, Jay Jenkins, Kharin Cain
- Producer: Needlz

I'm On One

I'm On One, by American hip-hop artist DJ Khaled, features Drake, Lil Wayne and Rick Ross. The song released on 20 May 2011, was nominated for Best Rap/Sung Collaboration at the 2012 Grammy Awards, eventually losing out to Kanye West's All the Lights.

- Released: 20 May 2011
- Album: We Are The Best Forever
- Label: We The Best, Terror Squad, Cash Money Universal Motown
- Length: 4:56
- Writers: Khaled, William Roberts, Dwayne Carter Jr, Noah Shebib, Aubrey Graham, Tyler Williams, Nikhil Seetharam
- Producers: T Minus, Nikhil, Noah Shebib,
- Music Video: Gil Green

The song went on to be certified triple platinum by the Recording Industry Association of America with sales of over 3 million and peaked at number one on both the US Rap Song and the Hot R&B/Hip-Hop Song charts and is DJ Khaled's most successful song to date. Directed by Gil Green, the music video was filmed at Drake's apartment at the Marquis Residences in downtown Miami, over the Memorial Day weekend of 26-27 May 2012.

In April 2013, Khaled brought Drake, Lil Wayne and Rick Ross back together on the gold certified single, No New Friends, the lead single from his seventh studio album, Suffering From Success. Drake co-directed the music video for the song.

Instagram

Champagnepapi is Drake's account name on Instagram, the popular photograph sharing application on the web.

International Creative Management

Drake joined International Creative Management in 2009 and the agency handled all his touring arrangements until he officially left in November 2011, when he went on to join the New York based William Morris Endeavor, which is the largest global talent agency. After leaving ICM, it was confirmed that ICMs Robert Gibbs would still be responsible for all the domestic (North America) bookings for Drake, with William Morris Endeavor responsible for all other worldwide bookings.

J

James LeBron

LeBron James is an American professional basketball player for the Miami Heat, and is a great friend of Drake, with the pair often seen together at award ceremonies and parties when their busy schedules allow. A fan from the early days, James hosted the release party for Drake's So Far Gone EP, which was held at the 6 Degrees nightclub in Toronto on 22 February 2009. James has even texted medical advice to Drake on how to handle his rehabilitation regime following the knee injury he originally sustained while playing basketball with friends, which he went on to further damage while performing on the 2009 America's Most Wanted tour with Lil Wayne. James has said of his friend:

> 'What we have is real family; it's not just because we are successful at what we do. We really care about one another on a day-to-day basis. Anytime you get a friend that can come and support you, in what you do, I respect that. Anytime I get free time, I try to support him as well.'

Drake's song Forever – featuring Kanye West, Lil Wayne and Eminem – was used as the background music to the LeBron James documentary *More Than A Game,* which was released in October 2009. The documentary follows LeBron's rise to fame and is accompanied by a soundtrack album featuring an all-star cast, with Stronger by Mary J Blige as the lead single. Released on 27 August 2009, Forever reached number one on the US Rap Song chart and was performed live on 31 January 2010 by Drake, Wayne and Eminem at the 52nd Grammy Award show, held at the Staples Center in Los Angeles.

The music video for the song, directed by Hype Williams features LeBron James, with photographs and video clips of him playing basketball from an early age.

Drake's character appeared in episode 7 of the animated series, *The LeBrons*, which aired on 24 May 2011.

Jay Z

Shawn Carter, aka Jay Z is an American rapper, record producer and entrepreneur from New York City. After years of performing with little success – selling his CDs from the car with no publishing deal – he finally co-created Roc-A-Fella records in 1995 and released the first of his 12 studio albums, Reasonable Doubt the following year. Since then he has sold over 50 million albums worldwide and has received 17 Grammy Awards. Jay has also furthered many an artists career including Kanye West, who produced his 2001 The Blueprint album. Drake has said that Jay Z was the artist who has inspired him more than anybody else and he has featured on a number of Jay Z's tracks.

He has also appeared on numerous tour dates, joining Jay Z on stage at the Air Canada Centre in Toronto on 31 October 2009, for his first performance since he had surgery on his knee. In front of a sold-out crowd of 20,000, Jay cued the introduction to Successful, promoting instant recognition and a great reception from the crowd as Drake strolled onto the stage to perform his hit song in front of his home crowd. Jay Z later joined Drake and his OVO crew at a Queens Street bar in the city, were Jay spent some time behind the bar serving cocktails to the crew.

In 2010, Drake appeared with Jay Z and Eminem on their Home from Home tour in New York (see **Photographs**) and opened for Jay on the European leg of his Blueprint 3 tour in Manchester and Birmingham, on 7 and 8 June respectively. (see **Blueprint 3**)

On 2 August 2010, Jay Z joined Eminem as surprise guests at Drake's first OVO festival in Toronto, with Jay Z performing his Grammy Award winning single, Run This Town. The duo have also collaborated together on a number of tracks, including Off That, from Jay's 2010 Blueprint 3 album, with Jay returning the favour by appearing on Light Up, from Drake's debut studio album, Thank Me Later.

In August 2012, Drake passed Jay Z's record of nine number one hits on Billboard's Hip-Hop/R&B Song chart, after No Lie gave Drake his 10th number one on the chart. It took Drake just 3 years and 1 month to achieve the feat, since Best I Ever Had hit top spot.

The two continue to have a friendly relationship and Drake was seen serving drinks to Jay and his wife Beyonce, during the NBA All-Star basketball game, at the Toyota Center in Houston, Texas in February 2013. Later that year, Drake released a song called Girls Love Beyonce and Jay Z featured on Pound Cake/Paris Morton Music 2 from Drake's third studio album, Nothing Was the Same, released on 24 September 2013.

Early in 2013, Jay Z and Beyonce followed Big Jon Platt (see **Platt Jon**) from EMI Publishing to Warner/Chappell, signing a publishing deal covering his music from 2008 and all future music. His album, Magna Carta Holy Grail was certified platinum three days before the official release date of 7 July 2013, due to an unprecedented promotional deal with the technology company Samsung. The deal involved 1 million advanced copies being given away to mobile phone and tablet users before the official release of the album, the first deal of its kind. The album went straight to number one on all American record charts.

J-Mac

Men's barber Jason Macaraig hails from Toronto and has been cutting hair for over 15 years. He has built up a long list of celebrity clientele such as Nas, Mack Maine, J Cole, Trey Songz, French Montana and Drake.

Working out of the Forum Barber Parlour on Yonge St, Toronto, 'J-Mac' was first introduced to Drake in 2004 by mutual friend Nicholas 'Niko' Carlino. Niko persuaded Drake to visit the barber shop to get his hair cut because he was so embarrassed hanging out with Drake who at that time had a terrible 'fro'. After some debate about what style he wanted, J-Mac went to work and performed his magic, with Drake saying that when he left the shop he felt reborn. Macaraig continues to be Drake's personal barber to this day. (see **Afro**)

Macaraig, who graduated as a physiotherapist assistant in 2005, is determined to expand his barbershop Get Faded and has created a mixtape called Clean Cuts, which features a couple of tracks from Drake, Dreams Money Can Buy and Headlines. He has also commissioned a barbershop inspired single called I Get Faded, which was produced by Boi-1da.

In 2012, Macaraig formed an alliance with Red9ine Tattoo parlour and works out of their Toronto shop, in addition to his regular residency.

Juno Awards

The Juno Awards are named in honour of Pierre Juneau, the first President of the Canadian Radio, Television and Telecommunications Commission. The awards are presented annually to Canadian musicians, artists and bands to acknowledge artistic and technical achievements in all aspects of Canadian music and are televised from a different location each year. The nominees are determined by sales during the qualifying period, usually the previous calendar year. Drake is especially proud to be nominated for a Juno, seeing it as recognition of his talent from his home country and his continual pride in being a Canadian.

In 2010, Drake won his first Juno Awards for Rap Recording of The Year – with So Far Gone – and as New Artist of the Year, beating his good friend Justin Bieber, with whom he generously offered to share the award. (see **Photographs**) The pair later performed an acoustic version of Bieber's song Baby – the best selling song in US history – and Wavin' Flag with K'naan during the show.

In 2011, the awards were held in Toronto and Drake had the privilege of becoming the youngest host in the show's history on his home turf. The show which was televised from the Air Canada Centre on 27 March, was also the Juno's 40th anniversary. During the show Drake appeared in a hilarious spoof filmed from the New Horizons care home, where he is shown trying to teach the elderly residents to rap. He also wears a sweatshirt with Old Money – an obvious gag with Young Money – on the front and ends up surrounded by the residents, drinking champagne and throwing money in the air exaggerating the hip-hop life.

Drake has won four Juno awards from sixteen nominations in a variety of categories: Rap Recording of The Year twice, with So Far Gone in 2010 and Take Care in 2012; New Artist of the Year in 2010; and Video of the Year with HYFR in 2013.

Drake's producer and fellow Canadian Noah '40' Shebib was nominated for the Jack Richardson Producer of The Year Award for Marvin's Room and Take Care in 2012.

Drake's Juno Awards

Year	Recipient	Award	Result
2010	Drake	New Artist of the Year	Won
2010	So Far Gone	Rap Recording of the Year	Won
2012	Take Care	Rap Recording of the Year	Won
2013	HYFR	Video of the Year	Won

The 2014 award ceremony will be held at the MTS Centre Winnipeg, Manitoba on 30 March.

K

Khaled DJ

Khaled Bin Abdul Khaled, aka DJ Khaled, is an American record producer, rapper, record label executive and radio host. After years of producing other artists albums, he finally released his debut studio album in 2006, called Listenn... the Album with the lead single, Holla At Me featuring Lil Wayne. Success finally arrived for Khaled in 2007 with his second album We the Best, again featuring Lil Wayne, along with Birdman, Rick Ross and Young Jeezy, which reached number two on the US Billboard Top R&B/Hip-Hop and Rap Album charts.

In 2009, Khaled was appointed President of Def Jam South, the southern division of Def Jam Recordings, who have artists Rick Ross, Young Jeezy and Ludacris on its roster.

Drake first collaborated with Khaled on the single, Fed Up from Khaled's fourth studio album, Victory released in 2010, which Drake also helped to co-write. The following year, the duo collaborated again on the triple platinum certified, I'm On One from Khaled's fifth album, We the Best Forever. The album was released onto the Terror Squad, Cash Money, Universal and We the Best labels on 19 July 2011. I'm On One was nominated for Best Rap/Sung Collaboration at the 2012 Grammy Awards and is Khaled's most successful single to date with sales of over 3 million.

During his career, Khaled has worked with almost every major artist in rap and hip-hop, and released his seventh studio album on 22 October 2013.

Khaled named the album Suffering From Success, after he had visited his doctor about the bald spot on his beard and received a diagnosis that it was due to him 'suffering from success'.

In April 2013, Khaled reformed the crew who featured on his hit single I'm On One – Drake, Rick Ross and Lil Wayne – with the release of the lead single from the album, No New Friends, produced by Boi-1da and '40'. Drake also co-directed the music video with Colin Tilley.

Khatib-El Oliver

Oliver El-Khatib was born in Toronto in 1986 and is part Lebanese-Scandanavian. He grew up travelling between Toronto and London and went to the same high school as Noah '40' Shebib, with the pair both meeting Drake at around the same time. El-Khatib has vast experience of fashion and clothing trends, having worked as a buyer and stylist for numerous Toronto street-wear stores and directing the Ransom catalogues.

He quickly progressed from advising Drake on his look and clothing style to becoming a close friend and manager. He also has responsibility for updating posts on the October's Very Own blog, where he keeps Drake's fans abreast of the latest clothing styles and music tastes. He still influences Drake's style and brand to this day, overseeing the OVO clothing line.

El-Khatib has also been credited with the artwork for Drake's So Far Gone EP and as a co-writer of The Resistance, the third track from Drake's debut album, Thank Me Later. With a good ear for music he introduced Drake to the music of The Weeknd, who went on to feature on Crew Love and perform at the OVO Festival and Francis and the Lights, who opened for Drake on his Away From Home tour in 2010.

Drake gives credit to El-Khatib on the sleeve credits from the album, Thank Me Later and has said of his friend:

> 'He has progressed from being my friend, who used to advise me on how to dress, to a guy who came up with the artwork for So Far Gone, he has a creative brain and he's become one of my managers.'

k-os

The Canadian rapper/singer Kevin Brereton, aka k-os, opened for Drake on his first headlining Away From Home tour, playing to various North American college campuses between April and May 2010. (see **Away From Home Tour**)

Brereton has stated that the acronym k-os originally stood for Kevin's Original Sound, and is always spelled lower case to appear less aggressive, in contrast to other rappers who spell their rap names in capital letters. Playing a mixture of genres from hip-hop, rap, rock and reggae, like Drake he performs with a live band when touring.

Brereton is credited as a musician, writer and producer on all of his five studio albums to date. Drake has said that k-os is someone he idolises and 'someone who I think is one of the greatest artists, period, and he's someone I really look up to.'

In August 2010, Drake featured on the k-os single Faith, from the mixtape Anchorman, which they laid down while they were touring together on the Away From Home tour. The duo collaborated again in 2011 with The Faith Part 2, produced by J.U.S.T.I.C.E League.

The Producers

Noah '40' Shebib & Matthew 'Boi-1da' Samuels

Drake often wears an earpiece in honour of Aaliyah when performing. Also note the jacket from his OVO clothing range

Hot 97 Who's Next show at
SOB'S in New York on 26 May
2009

Performing with Jay Z at the 2010 'Home & Home' concert in New York

Drake with his
Manager Cortez
Bryant

Drake with Lil Wayne at the BET Awards 2011

Drake with his mother at the 53rd Grammy Awards in 2011

Performing Headlines at the 2011 American Music Awards at the Nokia Theatre in Los Angeles

Drake gives the thumbs up on landing at Toronto Pearson Airport on 29 June 2010, to promote Virgin America's new Toronto service. The pLane nicknamed 'Air Drake' was emblazoned in the artwork for Thank me Later.

Drake performing at the BMI Unsigned Urban Showcase, in Austin Texas in April 2010, DJ Future the prince can be seen on the decks in the background

On the set of the 2013 film Anchorman 2; The Legend Continues where Drake had a cameo role

Drake with his 2010 New Artist & Rap Recording of the Year Juno Awards

Drake with the 2012
MTV Video Music
Award for HYFR

L

Lee Jade

Jade Lee is the girlfriend Drake mentions in his song Karaoke. The girl he called his first love and the one he wanted to marry who moved to Atlanta to pursue a career in wedding planning. Lee is the owner of a successful event company in Atlanta called Love Lee Events. On 20 May 2012, the pair where photographed together at the Velvet room in Atlanta, after Drake had performed at the Aaron Amphitheatre at Lakewood, during his Club Paradise Tour.

Lemoine Yoann

French graphic designer, singer-songwriter and director Yoann Lemoine, directed the music video for Drake's hit single, Take Care featuring Rihanna. The video was released on 6 April 2012 on MTV and Drake's OVO blog. Lemoine's previous work has included the music videos for Katy Perry's Teenage Dream, Taylor Swift's Back To December and Lana Del Ray's Video Games.

Les Miserables

Les Miserables was one of the first stage productions the young Aubrey Graham performed in after joining the Young People's Theatre in Toronto. He remembers 'Les Mis' as the first show that people came to see, liked and actually clapped because they enjoyed the performance and not because it had finished! During the show he performed one of his first public solo singing roles.

Light Dreams & Nightmares Tour

An official announcement on 29 July 2010 identified the venues for the Light Dreams & Nightmares tour, which followed hot on the heels of Drake's Away From Home tour, which had concluded just two days previously at the Vancouver Center for Performing Arts.

Somewhat appropriately, the Light Dreams & Nightmares tour opened in Miami, Florida on 20 September 2010 – Drake had just recently bought a home there – and was primarily used in support of the release of his debut studio album, Thank Me Later in June that year. The whole tour was staged in the US before he completed the rescheduled Away From Home European dates, which were cancelled due to his mother requiring surgery. Virginia hip-hop duo Clipse were originally due to be the chief supporting act throughout the tour, but Drake eventually decided to have his fellow Young Money artist Tyga as opening support act.

Some of Drake's pals from the hip-hop world joined him on stage during the tour. They included Mack Maine, Ne-Yo, Birdman, Fabolous, Rick Ross and Nicki Minaj, who made an appearance on 4 November at the Gibson Amphitheatre, LA. The biggest thrill for fans occurred when Jay Z strolled onto the Radio City Music Hall stage in New York, on Wednesday 29 September to perform their Thank Me Later collaboration Light Up and his own hit, Onto the Next One.

The tour was also noticeable for Drake's continued use of t-shirts in support of his friend Lil Wayne. The Young Money Entertainment boss was serving a one-year sentence for possession of a weapon and Drake often wore a 'Free Lil Wayne' t-shirt and asked the crowd to chant 'Free Wayne!' during the shows. Wayne made his first public performance since his release from prison – after serving 8 months of his sentence – during the final leg of the tour at The Joint, inside the Hardrock Hotel in Las Vegas, on Saturday 6 November.

Wayne hit the stage part way through Miss Me, with the capacity crowd immediately erupting with applause

The tour, which was sponsored by the telecommunications company AT&T was considered a huge success for Drake with all of the reviews from the music industry magazines favourable. Drake said prior to the tour:

> 'I'm gonna' do an hour and 45 minutes, for me that is crazy. I have trouble with the records I have just doing an hour and 15. If I do 75 minutes it means I have to cut out Miss Me, Light Up, and Money to Blow, records people want to hear. It's gonna' be a real interesting tour. I'm adding all the stuff from Thank Me Later. I've also got backing singers now to make stuff sound sweeter. I want people to walk away and say that was a great show; it was a fun time.'

Light Dreams & Nightmares Tour Venues:

September
09-20: Miami, FL. James L Knight Center
09-21: Miami, FL. James L Knight Center
09-23: Jacksonville, FL. Times Union Center
09-24: Tampa, FL. USF Sun Dome
09-28: New York, NY. Radio City Music Hall
09-29: New York, NY. Radio City Music Hal

October
10-01: Vesta, NY. Binghamton University
10-02: Washington, DC. Dar Constitutional Hall
10-03: Washington, DC. Dar Constitutional Hall
10-06: Atlanta, GA. Fox Theatre Atlanta
10-12: St Louis, MO. Fabulous Fox Theatre
10-13: Chicago, IL. The Chicago Theatre
10-14: Chicago, IL. The Chicago Theatre
10-16: Bloomington, IL. US Cellular Coliseum

October continued :
10-17: Dekalb, IL. NIU Convocation Center
10-19: Detroit, MI. Fox Theatre Detroit
10-21: Wallingford, CT. Toyota Presents the Oakdale Theatre
10-22: Philadelphia, PA. Wells Fargo Center
10-25: Boston, MA. TD Garden
10-26: Lowell, MA. Tsongas Center UMass
10-29: Houston, TX. Reliant Arena
10-30: New Orleans, LA. Voodoo Experience
10-31: Grand Prairie, TX. Verizon Theatre

November
11-02: Denver, CO. Wells Fargo Theatre
11-04: Universal City, CA. Gibson Amphitheatre
11-06: Las Vegas, NV@The Joint

Drake's first headlining tour of Europe – which included the cancelled Away From Home shows – opened in Glasgow, Scotland on 5 January 2011, featuring special guest and Roc Nation artist J Cole. The European tour concluded at the Forest National Club in Brussels, Belgium on 23 January 2011.

European Legs:

01-05: Glasgow, UK. O2 Academy
01-07: London, UK. Hammersmith HMV Apollo
01-08: London, UK. Hammersmith HMV Apollo
01-12: Manchester, UK. UK O2 Apollo
01-14: Birmingham, UK. The NIA
01-16: Berlin, Germany. Columbiahalle
01-19: Amsterdam, Holland. Heineken Music Hall
01-21: Paris, France. Zenith
01-23: Brussels, Belgium, Forest National Club

Love Me

Love Me is the third single from Lil Wayne's 2013 album, I Am Not A Human Being 2, his 10th studio album. The single, which features Drake and Future, was certified platinum by the RIAA with sales of over 1 million copies and reached number nine on the US Billboard Hot 100. The music video directed by Hannah Lux Davis, was premiered on 14 February 2013 on the hip-hop urban music video show, *MTV Jams*.

- Released:18 January 2013
- Album: I Am Not A Human Being 2
- Label: Young Money, Cash Money, Universal Republic
- Length: 4:15
- Writers: Dwayne Carter, Aubrey Graham, Navvadius Wilburn, Michael Williams
- Producer: Mike WiLL Made it
- Music Video: Hannah Lux Davis

M

Made Darkie

Darkie Made is a graphic artist from Toronto who designed the artwork for the single, Best I Ever Had. The original artwork for the single had featured a computer file with a plain white background, possibly trying to pay homage to the internet and its importance to Drake in the early days especially when he was uploading his mixtapes onto his MySpace page. However on its release, the artwork was deemed as too obscure by iTunes, so Made re-designed a new cover for the single. Made said of his work on So Far Gone:

> 'The most rewarding project of any of Drake's work I've done. That was just so unexpected, I had no idea he was gonna' blow up like that. It's not even like I got to hear So Far Gone before anyone else.'

He went on;

> 'I downloaded it at the same time as the rest of the world did. They just hit me up saying 'We need artwork, can you do it?' I said 'of course' and the monster grew from there. My artwork went from never being seen to being on the side of an airplane, when Virgin advertised their Toronto link, which is super humbling. I want to thank the OVO crew for that opportunity. It has exposed me to people worldwide and now people I really look up to have seen my artwork.'

Made went on to design the artwork for Drake's first studio album, Thank Me Later, which eventually ended up on the side of an Airbus A320 advertising Virgin America's new Toronto service. (see **Thank Me Later/Virgin America** and **Photographs**) He was also involved in the design of the cover for the third single from the album Miss Me, featuring Lil Wayne.

Make Me Proud

Released onto the OVO blog on 13 October 2011, 3 days before the official release date, Make Me Proud is the second single from Drake's second studio album, Take Care. Featuring Young Money associate Nicki Minaj, the single was certified platinum by the Recording Industry Association of America with sales of over 1 million.

The single reached number one on the US Hot R&B/Hip-Hop Song and the US Rap Songs charts, staying at number one on the Rap Songs chart, for 15 consecutive weeks.

- Released:16 October 2011
- Album: Take Care
- Label: Young Money, Cash Money, Universal Republic
- Length: 3:40
- Writers: Aubrey Graham, Onika Maraj, Tyler Williams, Nikhil Seetharam, Noah Shebib
- Producer: T Minus, Nikhil Seetharam

Mandler Anthony

Anthony Mandler is an American music video director from Los Angeles, who since directing his first music video – in 2000 for 8Ball & MJG – has directed numerous videos for some of the most popular artists of recent years.

Included in his extensive portfolio of artists are Rihanna, Beyonce, Jay Z, Nicki Minaj and of course Drake. The artist he has collaborated with the most has been Rihanna, starting with the video for her single Unfaithful in 2006 and ending with Diamonds in 2012, fourteen music videos in total.

Mandler has directed four of Drake's music videos to date since the first, Find Your Love in 2010. Drake has also featured on Mandler's video for the Mary J Blige single, The One from the previous year.

Anthony Mandler's Music Videos featuring Drake

Year	Artist	Single	Featuring
2009	Mary J Blige	The One	Drake
2010	Drake	Find Your Love	
2010	Drake	Over	
2010	Drake	Miss Me	Lil Wayne
2010	Drake	Fancy	TI Swiss Beatz

Man of the Year

GQ is an American monthly magazine which focuses on men's fashion, culture and style and Drake was named 'Breakout of The Year' at their, Men of the Year award ceremony held in Los Angeles on 17 November 2010. Drake has appeared twice on the cover of the magazine – three times if you count December 2010 were he was one of multiple cover stars – on April 2010 and June 2013.

Marvin's Room

Marvin's Room, taken from Drake's Take Care album, was released onto October's Very Own blog on 9 June 2011. The song, written by Drake, Noah Shebib and his guitarist Adrian Eccleston, was released before Headlines – the official first single from the album – and was certified gold by the Recording Industry Association of America with over 500,000 sales. The track, which was recorded at Marvin Gaye's old studio in Los Angeles, peaked in the top 10 on the Billboard Hot R&B/Hip-Hop Song chart and has been remixed by various artists including Lil Wayne on his mixtape, Sorry 4 the Wait.

- Released: 9 June 2011(OVO Blog)
- Album: Take Care
- Label: Young Money, Cash Money, Universal Republic
- Length: 3:17
- Writers: Noah Shebib, Adrian Eccleston, Aubrey Graham
- Producer: Noah Shebib
- Music Video: Hylene Alleyne

The atmospheric music video, directed by Hyghly Alleyne from The Weeknd's Toronto associates the XO crew, features Drake drunk inside a nightclub in reflective mood, telephoning an ex-girlfriend and telling her about his loneliness and his superiority over her present boyfriend. He tells her he wants to get back with her but without success, getting more inebriated as the beat gets gradually slower and the room continues to spiral. The video was generally well received by critics and fans alike.

Metalworks Studios

Metalworks Recording Studio, established in 1978 is situated in Mississauga, Ontario, Canada. Comprising six state of the art studios, Metalworks has been recognised as Canada's Studio of the Year for the 14th consecutive year at the Canadian Music Industry Awards. Artists such as Lil Wayne, Bruce Springsteen, Prince and Tina Turner have graced the premises and gold and platinum discs adorn the walls of the corridors at the studio, a testament to the studios success.

Drake has worked at the studios continually since his early breakthrough in 2008-9 and recorded the majority of his Take Care album there. On 1 March 2013, the studio accepted the double platinum award to commemorate 2,400,000 sales of Take Care. The album was number one on the Billboard chart and also won a Grammy Award for Best Rap Album of the year. Gil Moore, Founder and CEO of Metalwork Group said of Drake and his crew 'It's an honour to work with Drake and his team. They are like family to us.'

Chris Crerar, Studio Manager added, 'Congratulations to Drake and his crew for winning the Grammy for Best Rap Album of the Year with Take Care; we are honoured to have been part of the project.'

In 2013, DJ Khaled recorded his gold certified single, No New Friends featuring Drake, Rick Ross, and Lil Wayne at the Metalworks Studios.

Michele Chrisette

Chrisette Michele is a Grammy Award winning R&B singer-songwriter from New York. Drake appeared in the music video for Epiphany, the lead single from her 2009 album of the same name, released on the Def Jam label.

The pair worked together again the following year, both featuring on the Rick Ross single, Aston Martin Music.

Minaj Nicki

Nicki Minaj is a member of Young Money Entertainment and has collaborated with Drake on a number of singles, including their smash platinum certified hits, Moment 4 Life, from Minaj's Pink Friday album and Make Me Proud, from Drake's Take Care album. The Grammy Nominated single, Moment 4 Life is almost autobiographical about two kids who grow up in the same block and dream of making it as rappers. Eventually, they make it and they want to keep that 'Moment 4 Life'.

Born in Trinidad and Tobago in 1982, Onika Tanya Maraj lived with her Grandmother for the first five years of her life, before rejoining her parents in the Queens Borough of New York, where they had emigrated to find work and a better life. Attending elementary school and middle school, where she played the clarinet, she graduated from LaGuardia High School, which specialises in music and visual and performing arts, intent on being an actress. After failing to make an impact as an actress she began rapping in a group called the Hood$tars, releasing a number of moderately successful songs, but impatient for success she eventually left to go solo. After uploading songs onto her MySpace page she was approached by Fendi, the CEO of Dirty Money Entertainment, who became her manager – it was Fendi who convinced Maraj to change her stage name to Minaj   and put her onto his 2007 Come Up DVD. Her big break came after Lil Wayne heard her track from the DVD, purely because he wanted to hear himself on the tape and she was on directly after his song. After hearing Minaj's performance he immediately decided to sign her up to his Young Money Entertainment label. Drake and Minaj have had a similar background in the music industry;

They were both discovered after uploading their mixtapes onto the social networking site MySpace.

Minaj was discovered by Dirty Money CEO, Fendi and signed by Lil Wayne to his Young Money Entertainment label after he heard her music on The Come Up DVD. Similarly, Drake was signed by Lil Wayne after Wayne was introduced to Drake's music by Jas Prince, who heard Drake's mixtape on his MySpace page.

Both young rappers signed to Young Money Entertainment in 2009 and joined Wayne's successful America's Most Wanted Festival Tour of the same year, which grossed over $42 Million. They were also credited with song writing duties on the early Young Money Entertainment single Bedrock, from the We Are Young Money Entertainment compilation album, released on 14 November 2009.

Minaj has featured on an official remix of Drake's hit Best I Ever Had, which she included on her third mixtape, Beam Me Up Scotty, released 18 April 2008 on the Young Money Entertainment label. The mixtape also featured guest spots by Drake, Busta Rhymes, Lil Wayne and Gucci Maine. The two rappers caused some excitement in 2010 regarding their relationship, after Drake had tweeted that he and his Young Money collaborator had secretly married. After much press interest and speculation, the duo eventually had to hastily put out a tweet stating that it was all a joke and apologised to family and friends for any harm done.

Minaj has been busy in 2013, winning the award for Best Female Hip-Hop Artist at the BET Awards for the fourth consecutive year and has appeared on the American TV entertainment show, *American Idol* as a judge alongside Mariah Carey. Her third studio album is set for release in 2014, along with her first film, The Other Woman.

Miss Me

Miss Me is the third single from Drake's debut studio album, Thank Me Later. The single, featured Lil Wayne and peaked at number 15 on the Hot Billboard 100 and number two on the US Rap Song charts. The track was certified gold by the Recording Industry Association of America, with sales of over 500,000 copies.

- Released: 1 June 2010
- Album: Thank Me Later
- Label: Young Money, Cash Money, Universal Motown
- Length: 4:26
- Writers: Dwayne Carter, Aubrey Graham, Matthew Samuels
- Producer: Matthew Samuels
- Music Video: Anthony Mandler

Produced by Matthew 'Boi-1da' Samuels, the song was originally produced by rapper Bun B, featuring Drake for his album Trill OG. Bun explains:

> 'We were at Takeover studios and over two days we recorded it for my project; it was called the All Night Long hook. Then Wayne heard it and wanted to get on it, but eventually Drake asked if he could have the record back for his album.'

The original track featuring Bun B, is now known as the OG mix and was released onto the internet in 2010.

Mixtape

A mixtape is a simple and cheap method for an artist to put together a compilation of music, either onto a cassette tape or a CD format. The idea originally gained popularity as a means to sample popular songs without paying royalties to the original artists due to the tapes being given away for free. It allows new artist's to gain free publicity and gives the fans a chance to compare their flow and word play with the original. Through his earnings from *Degrassi: The Next Generation* and with financial help from his Uncle Steve, Drake funded his first two mixtapes and uploaded them to the social media site MySpace. His first mixtape of self-penned verses, Room for Improvement was released in 2006 shifting a respectable number of copies.

But it was after releasing his second mixtape, Comeback Season in 2007 which earned him air-play in the US that really helped to propel Drake into the global market. This was primarily due to the single and music video for Replacement Girl, again funded by his uncle, which made it onto BET's cable network video show. It was after he had uploaded his mixtapes onto the social networking site that Jas Prince heard about the young Canadian rapper and introduced his music to Lil Wayne. Drake had also included a remix of Wayne's Man of the Year on the mixtape.

His third mixtape, So Far Gone with 18 tracks, was released on 13 February 2009, and sees Drake drifting effortlessly from rapping to singing. Two tracks were eventually released as singles from the following EP, Successful, featuring Trey Songz and Best I Ever Had. The mixtape received critical acclaim from both the professional critics and fans alike, with MTV calling it the hottest mixtape of 2009.

Moment 4 Life

Moment 4 Life, is a song by American rapper Nicki Minaj from her debut 2010 studio album, Pink Friday featuring Drake. The song – produced by Drake's close Toronto associate Tyler 'T-Minus' Williams – was nominated for a Grammy Award for Best Rap Performance in 2012. Drake had previously worked with his fellow Young Money Entertainment artist Minaj on Up All Night, from his debut studio album, Thank Me Later.

- Released: 7 December 2010
- Album: Pink Friday
- Label: Young Money, Cash Money, Universal Motown
- Length: 4:39
- Writers: Onika Maraj, Aubrey Graham, Tyler Williams, Nikhil Seetharam
- Producer: T-Minus
- Music Video: Christopher Robinson

Minaj, Drake and Williams are credited as writers of the single, which reached number one on both the US Rap Song and Hot R&B/Hip-Hop Song charts, being certified platinum with sales of over 1 million. The duo performed the song in public for the first time at the Hammerstein Ballroom, New York City on Thursday 25 November 2010, at Hot 97's Thanksgiving Party. The party was also the official launch day of Minaj's debut studio album, Pink Friday.

The music video for Moment 4 Life was directed by American film director Chris Robinson, who has previously worked with Alicia Keys, Jay Z and Lil Wayne. The video showcases all of Minaj's alter ego's such as Martha Zolanski, Roman and Shady with the finale seeing Minaj and Drake sharing a wedding kiss on the stroke of midnight.

Money to Blow

Money to Blow is the third single from American rapper Birdman's fourth studio album, Priceless and features Drake – using auto tune which alters vocal pitch – and Lil Wayne. The song reached number two on both the US Billboard Rap Song and the Hot R&B/Hip-Hop Song charts and was certified platinum by the Recording Industry Association of America.

The music video for the song was directed by Gil Green and features diamonds, dollar bills and Lamborghini cars as the background for ostentatious wealth.

- Released: 8 September 2009
- Album: Priceless
- Label: Cash Money, Universal Motown
- Length: 4:22
- Writers: Bryan Williams, Aubrey Graham, Dwayne Carter
- Producer: Chris Gholson aka Drumma Boy
- Music Video: Gill Green

Morton Paris

Paris Morton is an American model from Jacksonville, Florida, who has appeared in numerous music videos for Yo Gotti and Nelly, with Drake naming his own version of Aston Martin Music after her. Shortly after Drake had featured on Rick Ross' Aston Martin Music from the album Teflon Don, he posted his own version of the song entitled Paris Morton Music onto his OVO blog. Missing from Drake's rap-only track was Ross' melody and Chrisette Michele's vocal. Drake's version also included unreleased verses which referenced a Grammy Award winning speech he planned to use and didn't throw away when he failed to win an award; fortunately he made use of it in 2013!

Paris Morton 2 featured as the outro on the album Nothing Was the Same in 2013.

Mother

Drake has a unique racial and religious background, with his mother Sandi Graham, a white Jewish-Canadian and his father Dennis Graham, an African-American. Sandi Graham, – nee Sher – is from Toronto, Ontario and the couple divorced when he was five years old. His mother has always been a major influence in his life and career, bringing him up in the Jewish faith as a single mother living in Forest Hill, an affluent Jewish suburb of Toronto. Ms Graham was a teacher by profession but she had to retire prematurely due to suffering from rheumatoid arthritis. Drake has often described his maternal family as being very musical and artistic with involvement in the acting and art community scene in and around Toronto.

Throughout his teenage years his mother had always ensured that her son had observed the Jewish High Holy days such as Hanukkah and Yom Kippur. In keeping with Jewish practices when he was 13 years of age, a Bar Mitzvah was held for him at an Italian restaurant in Toronto.

Ms Graham has an extremely close relationship with her son, as evidenced by the cancellation of Drake's Away From Home European tour in 2010, owing to her requiring surgery on her spine. While Drake was on the American leg of the tour, his mother was losing weight rapidly and after diagnosis it was found that she had a problem with the vertebrae in her spine, which was affecting her neck and head movements which would require immediate surgery. Affectionately known as 'Mama Graham' by Drake and his fans, the situation became very precarious as her condition could have potentially paralysed her for life.

With the situation worsening, it quickly became apparent that surgery would be needed much earlier than anticipated and the tour was cancelled, with Drake flying home immediately to support his mother. The night before the surgery to correct her spine, he tweeted a message of support to his mother asking his fans to pray for her.

Despite the surgeons name being Dr Failings, the operation was a complete success and Drake described the Doctor as doing 'an incredible job.' Within weeks his mother started swimming to build up her strength and stamina, and she went on holiday to Rome to recuperate, paid for by her relieved son, making excellent progress. Shortly after the operation she accompanied Drake to the Grammy Awards ceremony in Los Angeles on 31 January 2011.

Drake has always acknowledged the impact his mother has had on his life and career; she regularly used to help out by packaging and posting out his early mixtapes to his fans. When questioned on his lyrics and word play, he has said that it was through his mother's encouragement for him to say simple things in a more original way that had him spend hours searching for more descriptive words to use in order to impress her, which now shows in his music She is also a great scrabble player and the pair would also duel over the board, trying to find unusual words to win the game.

In 2012 at a graduation ceremony at Jarvis Collegiate Institute in Toronto, Drake finally received his diploma after spending 5 months studying. During his acceptance speech after being presented with his diploma, Drake – who had dropped out of high school – shared life lessons with his fellow students.

With his award in hand he dedicated the award to his mother thanking her for her continual support saying:

> 'This piece of paper, I'd like to dedicate to my mother because she's a retired teacher and always wanted me to graduate. I think I'll sleep a little better tonight knowing that I found a way to follow through.'

MTV Video Music Awards

The MTV Video Music Awards recognise the top music videos of the year and it was at the MTV VMA awards, held at the Paramount Studios in Hollywood, California on 7 September 2008, that the world heard Lil Wayne shout out the relatively unknown Drake's name. While Leona Lewis was singing Nina Simeon's Please Don't Let Me Be Misunderstood, which Wheezy had sampled on Don't Get It – the first of his trio of melodies on the night – he rapped Drake's verse from Money to Blow. He finished his set with a shout out to the world, 'Drizzy Drake; I love you bwoy!' But unfortunately, Drake was stuck outside the arena, due to him not having the right pass, so he couldn't see the show or hear Wheezy's tribute. On 6 September 2012, after being nominated nine times over the years in different categories, Drake finally won an award – affectionately called moonmen – for MTV's Best Hip-Hop Video for HYFR. (see **Photographs**) While accepting his award, Drake brought fellow Young Money artists Lil Wayne, who provided a verse on the song, and Nicki Minaj onto the stage, and told the assembled audience:

> 'Well first of all obviously I gotta thank Lil Wayne because he killed the song. I gotta thank everybody from Young Money shout out to Toronto, One time! The video, it's about me being black and Jewish. I went to this house party one time and when I showed up there it was a bunch of kids and I ended up getting made fun of. So I want to dedicate this award to any kid that has ever had a long walk home by yourself, you know what I'm saying? This is for you man, we made it!'

The video, which was a tribute to his Jewish roots and background, featured a scene from a Bar Mitzvah, filmed inside Miami's Temple Israel. (see **HYFR**)

On 25 August 2013, at the awards evening held at Brooklyn's Barclays Center, NY, the video for Started From the Bottom received two nominations for Best Hip-Hop Video and Best Direction. Drake also performed two singles from his upcoming third studio album on the night, Started From the Bottom and Hold On We're Going Home.

Drake's MTV Award Nominations

Year	Nominated Work	Award	Result
2009	Best I Ever Had	Best New Artist	Nominated
2010	Find Your Love	Best Male Video	Nominated
2010	Forever	Best Hip-Hop Video	Nominated
2011	Moment 4 Life	Best Collaboration	Nominated
2012	Take Care	Video Of The Year	Nominated
2012	Take Care	Best Male Video	Nominated
2012	Take Care	Best Art Direction	Nominated
2012	Take Care	Best Cinematography	Nominated
2012	HYFR	Best Hip-Hop Video	**WON**
2013	Started From The Bottom	Best Hip-Hop Video	Nominated
		Best Direction	Nominated

MuchMusic Video Awards

The MuchMusic Video Awards are presented annually by the Canadian music video channel to honour the year's best music videos. Drake first attended the awards in 2009, where he gave an impromptu question and answer session with the public and industry hosts. In all, Drake has been nominated nineteen times, winning six awards in different categories.

In 2010, Drake won two awards for Cinematography of The Year and MuchVibe Hip-Hop Video of The Year with the music video for his song Successful. At the ceremony, Drake performed his single Over live on a specially constructed stage which was set up outside the MuchMusic Studios headquarters on St John Street. He was accompanied by his four piece band in front of thousands of ecstatic fans, who gave Drake a great home-coming reception.

In 2011, Drake won the International Video of the Year by a Canadian for Find Your Love. He also won one award from five nominations the following year for The Motto, which won the MuchVibe Best Rap Video award.

In 2013, he won a further two awards from five nominations with Director of The Year and Hip-Hop Video of The Year for his hit single, Started From the Bottom.

MySpace

Drake has been a member of MySpace since 1 June 2005 and below is his general info, as it appeared on his MySpace page www.myspace.com/thisisdrake. The total number of plays up to and including October 2013 is 241,715,012.

Genre: Hip-Hop/Rap

Location: Toronto, Ontario

Website: Drakeofficial.com

Record Label: ATF

Member Since: 01/06/2005

N

Nas

Nasir Jones, aka Nas is an American rapper who has released eight consecutive platinum and multi-platinum certified albums. His debut album, Illmatic was released in 1994 and is ranked as one of the greatest hip-hop albums of all time. His follow up album, It Was Written went straight to number one on the US Billboard 200 and Top R&B/Hip-Hop album charts. It was also certified double platinum by the Recording Industry Association of America. Drake has stated that when he was a teenager, he admired and appreciated Nas, Kanye West and Andre 3000. He said of the rapper:

> 'I really studied Nas and listened to his raps, but never really understood how he did it. I always wanted to understand how he painted those pictures and his rhyming bar structures, anything to let me understand, and to try to keep improving.'

In 2012, Nas released his critically acclaimed eleventh studio album Life is Good, which received four Grammy nominations for Best Rap Album, Best Rap Song, Best Rap Sung Collaboration and Best Rap Performance, without winning an award.

Nebby

Zineb Samir aka Nebby, is recognised as being Drake's first great love and it was she, for whom it is widely acknowledged that he wrote the hit single, Best I Ever Had.

Drake has also dropped her name into a number of his other songs, including Sooner Than Later and Look What You've Done, from the Take Care album.

They have remained friends and stay in touch, even though they are not now in a relationship. They were pictured together hitting the town in Times Square, New York on New Year's Eve 2012, with Drake wearing his $5000 limited edition OVO Chilliwack coat. Drake had performed on Carson Daly's New Year's special earlier that night.

Nelson Kadir

Kadir Nelson is an author, painter and artist originally from New Jersey, who now resides in Los Angeles. He designed the cover artwork for Drake's third studio album Nothing Was the Same, released on 24 September 2013. The album cover features two profiles of Drake as a young child and an updated shot, seemingly looking at each other. The two got together after Drake saw Nelson's artwork hanging on the walls of a recording studio in LA, he liked what he saw and got in touch.

New Orleans Bootlegger

In early February 2009, immediately after he had uploaded his third mixtape, So Far Gone onto his MySpace page, Drake realised that his music was being distributed to a wider audience from an unusual source and remembers:

> 'I was walking outside the W Hotel in New Orleans and right in front of me there was this guy selling mixtapes and one of them was So Far Gone. I couldn't believe it, but I wasn't even mad. You usually think you'll be mad when a bootlegger is doing his thing, but I just felt super excited.'

So Far Gone went on to be hailed as one of the best mixtapes ever released and was received favourably by critics, fans and 'bootleggers' alike.

Nickelus F

Nickelus F is an American rapper and song-writer from Richmond, Virginia. Since releasing his first mixtape, Anything You Can Do I Can Do Better in 2002, he has released a string of mixtapes including, Heathen, Thank You and R.A.R.E and is often touted as one of the most underrated rappers around. In 2007 Nickelus won the Black Entertainment Television's 'Freestyle Friday' seven weeks in a row.

He first collaborated with Drake when he featured on the songs, AM 2 PM, Money, A Scorpions Mind and S.T.R.E.S.S off Drake's 2006 mixtape, Room for Improvement. Drake has also acknowledged that Nickelus F was a huge influence on him in the early days and one of the reasons he began to rap.

In January 2013, the pair teamed up again on the single Number 15, from the Nickelus F free to download album, Vices produced by Jake One. The song is widely known as the 'hookah verse' due to Drake uploading a video in 2012 with him smoking shisha from a hookah pipe, with a new and at that time unheard of catchy tune playing in the background, which eventually became the hook for Number 15.

No Lie

Drake featured on the lead single No Lie, by American rapper 2 Chainz from his debut studio album, Based on a TRU Story, which was certified platinum by the Recording Industry Association of America with sales of over 1 million copies. The song became Drake's 10th to reach number one on the Billboard Hot R&B/Hip-Hop Song chart, overtaking Jay Z who had held the record with nine songs at the summit.

The music video was directed by Director X, who went on to direct the video for Drake's Started From the Bottom, the first single from his third studio album, Nothing Was the Same.

- Released: 8 May 2012
- Album: Based on a TRU Story
- Label: Def Jam
- Length: 3:59
- Writers: Michael Williams, Marquel Middlebrooks, Tauheed Epps, Aubrey Graham
- Producer: Mike WiLL Made It, Marz
- Music Video: Director X

Nothing Was the Same

Drake announced the title for his third studio album while he was being interviewed on the red carpet at the Grammy Awards ceremony held at the Staples Center, Los Angeles on 10 February 2013, where he picked up his first Grammy for Best Rap Album, with Take Care. The album, Nothing Was the Same, was eventually released on 24 September 2013 after missing the scheduled release date of 17 September, due in part to the difficulty in getting certain samples cleared.

- Released: 24 September 2013
- Album: Nothing Was the Same
- Label: OVO Sound, Young Money, Cash Money, Republic
- Length: 67:53
- Writers: Aubrey Graham, Noah Shebib, Matthew Samuels, Kanye West, Wayne Carter, Anthony Palaman,
- Producers: Shebib, Zombie, Boi-1da, Key Wayne, Hudson Mohawke, Majid Jordan, Nineteen85

Two weeks before the album dropped Drake joked to reporters that he and '40' had literally been camping out at the studio to enable the album to come to fruition.

On release, the album debuted at number one on the US Billboard 200 with first-week sales of 658,000 copies. It also debuted at number two on the UK Album chart, Drake's highest UK album chart position. In October 2013, the album was certified platinum by the Recording Industry Association of America with sales of over 1 million copies.

Singles from Nothing Was the Same Album

Title	Featuring	Release Date
Started From the Bottom		6 February 2013
Hold On, We're Going Home	Majid Jordan	7 August 2013
All Me	Big Sean	24 September 13
Pound Cake	Jay Z	30 September 13
The Language		29 October 2013
Too Much	Sampha	31 October 2013

The first single from the album, Started From the Bottom peaked at number two on both the R&B/Hip-Hop Song and the US Rap Song charts and was certified double platinum by the RIAA on 23 August. The second single, Hold On, We're Going Home, featuring Canadian duo Majid Jordan – who also co-produced the single – reached number one on the R&B/Hip-Hop Song chart and was Drake's highest charting song in the UK single chart peaking at number four. Majid Jordan are signed to Drake's OVO Sound Label.

The phrase 'Nothing Was the Same' had previously featured on the single 5AM In Toronto

The intro for the album, Tuscan Leather is named after a cologne by Thomas Ford and is Noah Shebib's favourite track off the album.

Kadir Nelson designed the cover art for the album which consisted of two oil paintings of Drake in profile, one as a child and another as he is now, with the two images facing each other.

O

October's Very Own (OVO)

October's Very Own, is the name given to Drake's official website, blog and clothing range. It is also the name by which his close team of friends and advisers are called. Named mainly due to Drake having his birthday in October, below are the main members of the OVO crew.

Noah '40' Shebib: Drake's producer and engineer has been with him from the Comeback Season mixtape days and has produced most of Drake's music since then. In the early days he served as road manager, keyboard player, roadie and even cash point, when he put up thousands of dollars to pay the bills while the duo where on the road for the So Far Gone tour in 2009. (See **Shebib Noah**)

Nicholas 'Niko' Carino: one of Drakes early friends from Toronto who started working with Drake selling his mixtapes at nightclubs. He encouraged Drake to get his afro cut which Drake has said changed his life and improved his confidence. Niko also joined Drake on the SFG tour helping out as roadie and general labourer. Drake calls him the brother he has never had and is one of his closest confidantes. (See **Carino 'Niko' Nicholas**)

Oliver El-Khatib: started out working in clothing stores in Toronto, before becoming Drake's fashion and creative manager, advising on everything from clothing brands, music and video composition. El-Khatib also updates the official OVO blog and was made Drake's manager in 2012. He also introduced Drake to the music of fellow Torontonian, The Weeknd. (See **Khatib-El Oliver**)

Offishall Kardinal

Kardinal Offishall, is known as Canada's hip-hop ambassador and is regarded as one of the country's best hip-hop producers. He featured on Rascalz's hit single Northern Touch, which won a Juno for Rap Recording of The Year in 1999. The song, from the album Cash Crop is generally identified as one of the most important individual songs in the history of Canadian hip-hop, helping to transform the genre from a largely ignored underground scene into a successfully viable commercial entity. The music video for the song was the first by Director X (as Little X), who has gone on to have a successful career in the industry, culminating in him directing the music video for Drake's 2013 hit, Started From the Bottom.

Offishall was one of Drake's favourite rapper/hip-hop artists, while he was growing up in Toronto. He remembers seeing him at Toronto's Yorkdale Mall one afternoon and being so in awe of him, due to it being the first time he had seen a star close up, that he never went over and said hello. The two eventually worked together on The Last Hope, a song off Drake's 2007 mixtape Comeback Season. Offishall also appeared at Drake's first OVO Festival in 2010 at the Molson Amphitheatre, Toronto.

Omen

Sidney 'Omen' Brown, the Grammy Award winning producer, has worked with Drake on a number of occasions. Their first collaboration occurred on the 2008 single, Overdosing on Life which featured Drake, Mickey Factz and Travie McCoy, from the album Be The Judge. Drake recorded his verse at The Remix Project recording studio assisted by Noah Shebib. Omen has also co-produced a number of tracks with Noah Shebib; Shut It Down, which was the eighth track from Drake's album Thank Me Later, featuring The-Dream and I'm Single from Lil Wayne's 2009 mixtape, No Ceilings.

Omen won the 2007 Grammy Award for Best Rap Album for his production work on the single, Tell It Like It Is, from Ludacris's double album, Release Therapy.

Ora Rita

Rita Ora is a British singer-songwriter who is signed to rapper Jay Z's Roc Nation record label. She came to the attention of Roc Nation after her manager informed them of this hot new talent singing in London bars and clubs. After hearing her music, she was invited to fly to New York to see Jay and the rest of the Roc Nation team and she was signed to the label in 2009. She made a cameo appearance on Jay Z's music video for his Young Forever single. Jay Z himself went to the New York City radio station Z100 on 24 February 2012 and introduced Ora's first official single, How We Do (Party) to the station's listeners.

Her debut album, Ora also included the UK lead single R.I.P. – a Drake penned song – which was originally intended for Rihanna's album Loud. Ora performed R.I.P. at the Manchester MEN arena on 1 April 2012, as support artist for Drake's Club Paradise tour. The duo had previously appeared together in the music video for Drake's 2010 hit Over, with Ora as his love interest. She eventually went on to release three singles from the Ora album, which have all reached number one in the British charts, the two mentioned above and Hot Right Now which featured DJ Fresh. Ora's second album is due for release in 2014.

Ora presented Drake with a vintage ring as a token of her friendship and thanks for his support in aiding her career, especially for giving her the hit R.I.P. But this simple act of friendship caused a storm in the press about who had actually given Drake the ring, with Rihanna's name constantly being mentioned.

When interviewed in London for his Club Paradise tour, Drake's aim was to dispel the rumours about who gave him the ring and he responded to questions that it was indeed Ora that she was a dear friend and the ring is one of his treasured items of jewellery.

Over

Over is Drake's first single taken from his debut studio album, Thank Me Later. The single was released on 8 March 2010, with Drake premiering the song on Toronto radio station Flow 93.5. In the song he directly addresses the downside to his new found fame and success.

The song, produced and co-written by Boi-1da was certified gold by the Recording Industry Association of America, with sales of over 500,000 copies and reached number one on the US Hot Rap Song chart. It was also nominated for the Best Rap Solo Performance at the 53rd Grammy Awards, eventually losing out to Eminem's quadruple platinum hit, Not Afraid.

- Released: 8 March 2010
- Album: Thank Me Later
- Label: Young Money, Cash Money Universal Motown
- Length: 3:53
- Writers: Noah Shebib, Aubrey Graham, Matthew Samuels, Nick Brongers
- Producer: Boi-1da, Al Khaaliq
- Music Video: Andrew Mandler

The music video was directed by Andrew Mandler and features Roc Nation artist Rita Ora as Drake's love interest. Ora went on to record the Drake penned hit single R.I.P.

OVO Festival Toronto

The OVO Festival is held around the first weekend in August each year to correspond with the Canadian 2-day Civic public holiday and is the culmination of Drake's ambition to reward his hometown fans for their constant support. The first show was held at the 17,000 seat Molson Amphitheatre on 1 August 2010. Drake called in some favours from his friends in the music industry to appear, with Jay Z – who also performed his hit Run This Town – and Eminem the main guest artists joining Drake on stage for a verse of Forever. With Mack Main, Young Jeezy, Rick Ross and fellow Toronto rapper Kardinall Offishall also appearing at the inaugural show.

On 31 July 2011 at the second OVO Festival, Drake brought out Stevie Wonder, who instead of performing the planned two songs as agreed, stayed and played a 30-minute set which included a sing-along with the crowd on My Cherie Amore, with Drake adding a freestyle. Also appearing on the show were Lil Wayne, who joined Drake and Rick Ross on stage to perform I'm On One, J Cole, Nas and fellow Torontonian and Drake protégé The Weeknd who performed Crew Love. The Weeknd, appeared at the Festival following his first live public performance the previous weekend at the Mod Club in Toronto.

The third OVO festival held on 5 August 2012, opened with The Weeknd, A$AP Rocky and 2 Chainz. Then dressed all in white Drake took to the stage to perform most of his hits including fan favourites, Over, November 18th, Underground Kings and Marvin's Room. The guest stars then appeared, French Montana and Rick Ross for Pop That, No Lie with 2 Chainz, Amen featured Meek Mill and Snoop Dogg joined Drake for Drop It Like Its Hot, before Nicki Minaj joined him on stage to perform their hit single, Make Me Proud.

During the show Drake revealed for the first time in public his 416 tattoo – the telephone code for Toronto city centre – to rapturous applause, again showing his love for his home city. Drake closed the night with Headlines.

Although headliner Frank Ocean's absence – due to a sore throat – meant the loss of an entire day, the fourth OVO Festival at the Molson Amphitheatre on Monday 5 August 2013, again did not disappoint. The evening started with Wale and James Blake opening the show. Drake then came onto the stage to perform Headlines, with The Weeknd joining him on stage to perform Crew Love, dispensing rumours of a falling-out between the pair due to The Weeknd signing to Republic Records. Drake then went in on 5AM In Toronto, Poetic Justice and Girls Love Beyonce.

J Cole and Miguel then hit the stage before Drake reappeared for a melody of his hits; Succesful, Uptown, Best I Ever Had and Over. Diddy and Mase then followed, before Drake introduced Kanye West who performed New Slave, and All Of the Lights before telling the crowd that without Drake putting pressure on them, he and Jay Z would never have made Watch the Throne and he wanted to pay his respects to him. The stars kept coming with legendary R&B group TLC making their OVO Festival debut with Waterfall and No Scrubs. Lil Wayne then closed the show, but before he left he pointed to Drake and addressing the sell-out 17,000 crowd he said 'Make some noise for what this man has accomplished and I'm happy to have been a piece of the puzzle.' It said it all.

OVO Sound

Created in 2012, OVO Sound is Drake's record label based in Toronto and is distributed by Warner Music Group. Canadian singer/rapper PartyNextDoor is the first artist to be distributed by the label, with Make A Mil the first single released from his self-titled mixtape. Drake featured on Over Here from the mixtape.

OVOXO

OVO or October's Very Own is the name of Drake's close group of friend's from Toronto and XO is The Weeknd's crew. XO are also Toronto based and consists of Hyghly Alleyne and Lamar Taylor, who have provided direction and the artwork for Drake's videos and albums. When the two groups collaborate together they use the anagram OVOXO as the musical and social combination of the two groups. Drake wore an OVOXO sweatshirt at the second OVO Festival in 2011.

P

PartyNextDoor

Toronto singer/rapper Jahron Braithwaite, aka PartyNextDoor is the first artist signed to Drake's OVO Sound Label. Drake released his self-titled mixtape onto the OVO SoundCloud in April 2013, with Drake tweeting his support for his 20 year old protégé. The first official track released from the mixtape was called Make A Mil – produced by '40' – with Drake featuring on the ninth track off the mixtape, Over Here.

PartyNextDoor is credited with background vocals on Drake's 2013 album Nothing Was the Same, and featured as guest artist on his Would You Like A Tour? of North America.

Personal Chef

Los Angeles born Kayla Greer – also known by her working name of 'Chef KayKay' – has been working in the food industry since attending the Los Angeles Trade Technical College in 2007. She was introduced to Drake by producer Chase N Cashe, who had booked her to cater for a party for 100 people and it was only on arrival that she learned it was Drake who was hosting the party at his LA mansion. She did such a great job that Drake asked her to exchange telephone numbers and after providing the catering for a couple of further parties, he asked her to be his personal chef when he and the OVO crew are in town.

Personal Trainer

Drake has employed personal trainer Jonny Roxx to keep him in shape, especially just prior to going on tour since 2011. Roxx, a well-known celebrity trainer has previously worked as fitness director at Habitual gym and with professional athlete Amir Johnson. Drake gives Roxx a name check on his single 5AM In Toronto, were he talks of pushing 'two plates' which refers to a weight usually placed on both ends of a bar to be bench-pressed, which Drake uses as part of his intensive training regime. The pair where photographed together on vacation in 2012, paragliding behind a speedboat.

Phantom Rolls-Royce

In 2008, Drake leased a Rolls-Royce Phantom using the money he earned from acting on *Degrassi: The Next Generation,* leasing the car because he did not have enough money to buy the car outright. He admits using the Phantom to build a facade for himself in and around Toronto, to show that he was somebody and to fit into the world of hip-hop. The car which he leased from an 'old dude looking for loose money' caused a lot of problems at home.

His mother thought the car was ostentatious and an embarrassment, due to the family struggling financially at that time. The car became such a problem for the family that Drake had to park the car away from his home in another street to avoid any further arguments. He has often talked about this time in his life – during the making of the So Far Gone mixtape – and the fact that his family were in a very dark place, with lots of crying and shouting at home. Drake makes reference about their financial predicament and his mother being embarrassed about him driving around in a Rolls-Royce, on the track Say What's Real, from the So Far Gone mixtape.

David Irvine, who lived on the street where Drake parked his car, actually posted about the car in 2008 on the website 'Bentley Spotting'.

> 'Two summers ago there was a mysterious Phantom on my street. I did post a picture of it on this site some time ago. It would turn up very early every morning and as the sun set would disappear, heading in the downtown direction at 7pm or 8pm. Sometimes in the dawn light as I returned from my morning run, I'd see the driver exit the vehicle and I'd bid him a 'Good Morning'. None of the neighbours seemed to know who he was, but the rumour was he was some up and coming DJ, Rapper or Club owner or maybe even something more sinister.'

Philanthropy

Drake is known for his philanthropic interests and his social conscious and awareness. This is mainly due to his mother's influence and he has always been aware of the inequalities in the world from an early age. Now owing to his success he can finally put his fame to good use and help to raise awareness of specific issues close to his heart. One of the first public examples of Drake's awareness of environmental issues occurred on his first headlining Away From Home tour of university campuses in 2010. Drake show-cased a tented 'Eco-Village' which assisted in educating his fans on green technology, student carbon-offset programs and eco-friendly solutions to some of the world's climate change problems.

In January 2010, he joined 50 fellow musicians to record a tribute single called Wavin' Flag, to help raise money for the relief fund after the Haiti earthquake devastation, with the single going straight to number one in the Canadian charts. Other examples included Drake's 2010 Light Dreams and Nightmares tour, when a portion of the proceeds from every ticket sold from the tour went to the Friends of the Music Therapy Endowment Fund, at the Hospital for Sick Children in Toronto, of which he is an ambassador.

On one of his regular visits to the hospital he made one girl's dream come true by handing his mobile over for her to talk with Justin Bieber. Drake's OVO Festival also benefits Jake's House for Autism and the MS Society of Canada.

In 2011, Drake received the Allan Slaight Award, which is presented to a young Canadian who is making a positive impact in the entertainment industry. The award comes with a $10,000 honorarium, which Drake chose to donate to Dixon Hall, a community based organisation, aiming to create positive opportunities in low-income neighbourhoods in and around Toronto.

On 15 September 2012 at the inaugural Kentucky Wildcats Alumni Charity Match held at the Rupp Arena, Drake coached the University of Kentucky men's basketball team to a win and also helped raise over $300,000 for local charities, with him presenting the cheque during the half-time interval.

Phonte

Phonte Coleman, along with Rapper Big Pooh and DJ/Producer Patrick Douthit, formed the hip-hop group, Little Brother in 2001. Drake has shouted out Little Brother on a number of occasions and has spoken about his respect for the group, acknowledging them as being a major influence on his early career. Drake has called the Little Brother's 2007 mixtape, Justus for All, hosted by DJ Mick Boogie, one of his favourite top five albums.

Phonte's track, Think Good Thoughts features on Drake's Comeback Season mixtape released in 2007. The track featured Phonte on vocals and was produced by Douthit under his stage name 9th Wonder.

Drake has also worked with 9th Wonder on a track for his second studio album, Take Care but the track did not make the cut owing to a copyright issue with the producer. However, Drake remains optimistic about a further collaboration with Phonte in the future.

On 26 August 2011 at Hollywood's Pantages Theatre while on stage receiving the BMI Songwriter of The Year Award, Drake dedicated the award to Phonte, Kanye West and Andre 3000 for inspiring his music.

Platt 'Big Jon'

In 2009 at the June BET awards, EMI Music Publishing executive Big John Platt found himself in his usual work mode. The President of West Coast Creative/Head of Urban, signed rising star Drake to a publishing deal in the artist's dressing room at the Los Angeles, Shrine Auditorium. A self-confessed work junkie who works all hours of the day and night to get the job done, Platt had previously flown to Canada after hearing Drake's mixtape, So Far Gone so that he could spend some time with Drake and watch him perform. He has said about the trip:

> 'We just hung out together all day and after we talked, I soon knew that he was the real deal, the whole package, with his music, lyrics and his flow he's got everything.'

The 6' 8" Platt hails from Montbello, Denver, Colorado and he started work in the entertainment industry as a DJ. He had a regular Saturday night residency at Norman's nightclub in his home town, before leaving for LA and world domination. Joining EMI in 1995 as the creative manager, he signed his first artist Jay Z in 1996 and went on to sign some of the biggest names in urban music including Kanye West, Usher, Beyonce and Ludacris. Jay Z credits Platt with giving him his first number one, with the smash hit song, Empire State of Mind with Alicia Keys.

Drake credited Platt for metaphorically 'saving his life' on the sleeve credits for his second studio album, Thank Me Later. Drake acknowledges that Big Jon had probably saved his life, due to him signing to EMI. He had stated that at the time he was in a bad place and that if he hadn't signed a recording contract who knows what might have happened to him and his career in the music industry.

Platt left EMI in June 2012 after 17 years at the company and under his creative guidance, EMI Music Publishing were the Billboard Publisher of the Year for the previous 12 years, and had won the ASCAP Rhythm & Soul Award for Publisher of the Year for 17 years in a row. He joined the rival organization, Warner/Chappell Music as President of North America Creative based in Los Angeles, and will assist in helping to shape future company strategy. Jay Z followed Platt to Warner/Chappell the following year with a publishing deal covering his music since 2008 and all future music.

Poetic Justice

Released on 13 January 2013, Poetic Justice is the third song from American hip-hop artist Kendrick Lamar's debut studio album, Good Kid MADD City and featured a verse from Drake. The single sampled Janet Jackson's Any Time Any Place and although it was certified gold with sales of 500,000 copies by the Recording Industry Association of America, it failed to reach the top five in any chart listings.

- Released: 13 January 2013
- Album: Good Kid MAAD City
- Label: Top Dawg, Aftermath, Interscope
- Length: 5:00
- Writers: Kendrick Lamar, Elijah Molina, Aubrey Graham, Janet Jackson, James Harris, Terry Lewis
- Producers: Scoop DeVille
- Music Video: Lil Homie, Dave Free Dangerookipawaa

Pop That

Pop That, is the first single from American rapper Karim Kharbouch's – aka French Montana – debut album, Excuse My French. Featuring Drake, Rick Ross and Lil Wayne, the song was certified platinum by the Recording Industry Association of America with sales of over 1 million copies and peaked at number two on both the US Hot R&B/Hip-Hop Song and the US Rap Song charts.

- Released: 15 June 2012
- Album: Excuse My French
- Label: Bad Boy Interscope
- Length: 5:04
- Writers: Karim Kharbouch, Rick Ross, Aubrey Graham, Wayne Carter, Anthony Norris
- Producer: Anthony Norris
- Music Video: Parris

Poverty

When Drake was 16 years old his father was incarcerated in prison for another short sentence. Owing to the long distance – and Drake being unable to travel alone – the pair communicated through calls made by Drake's father from the prison telephone.

During one of these conversations Drake's father introduced him to one of his prison friend's called Poverty, a young guy aged around 20, who was a budding rapper. During the numerous calls from prison his father – who knew of his son's interest in writing and rapping songs – would often hand the phone over to Poverty and he and Drake would rap to each other for a few minutes over the phone. When his father was eventually released from prison, Drake unfortunately lost contact with his unusual rap collaborator.

Prince 'Jas' James

James 'Jas' Prince Jr, has been widely acknowledged as being responsible for discovering Drake and introducing him to Lil Wayne and ultimately in becoming a Young Money/Cash Money recording artist. Prince, a Texas talent scout had first heard Drake's music after searching through social networking sites while looking for new musical talent for his Young Empire Entertainment label. It was on MySpace that Prince first heard Drake's music, after he had put up four of his songs and kept rotating them. After hearing the songs, Prince played Drake's mixtape to Lil Wayne while driving him in his car and after hearing just two tracks, Wayne told Jas to book Drake immediately onto the next flight to join him in Houston.

After introducing Drake's music to his father, James Prince, founder of Houston based Rap-a-Lot Records, and convincing him that Drake was the real deal, they immediately struck a deal with Lil Wayne, merging companies to co-manage him.

On Friday, 29 October 2010 at the Reliant Arena, Houston during his Light Dreams and Nightmares tour, Drake repaid his debt to Jas and pulled him onto the stage to hand him the keys to a new $250,000 Lamborghini sports car, then conducted the crowd to sing an impromptu happy 23rd birthday to Jas.

Promise

Promise Jason Jamal Sheperd, aka Promise is a Canadian hip-hop and soul singer-songwriter. Drake credits him for being one of the first people to recommend putting his music onto MySpace, as a format for reaching more people. Trey Songz had also suggested uploading his music onto MySpace, after the duo had worked together on his Comeback Season mixtape so Drake eventually decided to give it a try.

The songs he had uploaded were eventually heard by James 'Jas' Prince who was searching for fresh music talent for his label which led to Drake being introduced to Lil Wayne.

Drake has collaborated with Promise on a number of projects since they first met in 2007. He appeared on the singles, In My City and in 2008 You Got Me, also featuring American rapper Sacario. Also in 2007-8 Promise released two mixtapes, Kanye West Presents: Promise Vol 1 and 2 which showcased him with guest artists including West himself, John Legend and Drake. Drake featured on a song called This Way on the mixtape.

In 2009, Promise released the track, Letter to Drake featuring Mickey Factz. The song, which Promise had released just prior to Drake signing his lucrative record deal, was interpreted as an open letter to Drake warning him about the pitfalls of fame.

Promise and Drake both featured as part of 2K Sports' famed video game sound track NBA 2K11, which included a mixture of new upcoming bands and highly acclaimed artists such as Snoop Dogg. Drake with his single Over and Promise with his single, I'm Better Than You.

Punk'd

Drake featured on Series 9, Episode 11, of the hit American show *Punk'd*, which aired on 3 June 2012.

Punk'd, created, produced and hosted by American actor and comedian Ashton Kutcher consists of hidden cameras which capture celebrities completely unawares and often in embarrassing situations. The series initially ran from 2003-7 on MTV and resumed again in 2012.

In the show titled *The Big One,* Drake is set up by his friend and road manager, CJ Gibson and host Aston Kutcher. As part of the plot, Drake thinks he is going to meet the Vice President of the United States, Joe Biden and is picked up by bogus secret service agents in a people carrier to be taken to the meeting venue. On the journey to their destination, one of the agents even tells Drake to keep making good music and turns to him and says YOLO, which makes Drake smile to himself.

While waiting in the underground car park, apparently waiting to get security clearance to see the VP, a staged earthquake starts to erupt outside the building. The car Drake is sitting in starts to shake violently, along with the other parked cars, with fake masonry falling all around them. A heavily pregnant lady then appears with her anxious husband who is trying to get her to hospital, but unfortunately Drake's car is blocking their exit. Having no keys – the security men had left Drake and CJ in the car – Drake is unable to move the vehicle, so a search of the car is instigated by the husband trying to find a spare set. Unfortunately, he instead finds a dummy taser gun and then precedes to accidently taser his pregnant wife. After being 'tasered' his wife falls to the ground apparently in agony, with the cameras zooming onto Drake's face in close up, with him looking shocked and concerned.

At this stage Kutcher and his camera crew start to appear and as soon as Drake sees them he knows he's been had. After being Punk'd, Drake turns to the camera and says: 'At least it proves I've nearly made it, as it's only celebrities that get Punk'd.'

During the episode Drake said that he really thought he was going to die and even started texting his mother to tell her goodbye.

R

Radio Free Roscoe

Radio Free Roscoe is a Canadian television series, which was filmed in Toronto and first aired on 1 August 2003, ending on 27 May 2005 after 52 episodes.

Aubrey Graham appeared as a RFR caller in Season 1, Episode 11 of the show, with his good friend Ali Mukadam who played the character Ray. In the show the duo were trying to find dates for each other by eliminating various girls, according to their personality, looks and sense of humour, eventually failing miserably.

Ransom

After being invited to Houston after Jas Prince had introduced the duo, Drake and Lil Wayne recorded the now legendary underground freestyle Ransom, which featured both stars rapping a verse each. Ransom is the original version of I Want You Forever and a remix of Drake's song, Brand New. Ransom debuted on the popular hip-hop blog nahright.com on 4 September 2008, with Wheezy's scorching guest verse effectively vouching for Drake's legitimacy. More importantly, it was this collaboration that compelled Cortez Bryant to agree to sign as Drake's manager.

RapCity

RapCity is a Canadian television program that features on the MuchMusic cable channel. The show highlights new and vintage music from Canadian and American hip-hop artists.

Drake often listened to the station in his younger days and has said that 'Rap City is a legendary thing to me and was the only connection we had with the over the border culture and lifestyle. It helped form my own musical awareness.'

The show was re-launched on 13 January 2011, with new host and Drake's friend Tyrone 'T-RexXx' Edwards. Drake was honoured to be the first guest for the new show, but he had to pre-record the interview on 1 January, at 5am for transmission on the opening show. This was due to Drake having to catch a flight later that day to start the European leg of his Light Dreams and Nightmares tour at the O2 Academy in Glasgow on 5 January 2011. The hour-long interview featured Drake answering a number of questions about his early life, musical influences and future ambitions, with his producer Noah '40' Shebib in attendance.

The show currently airs live on Thursdays at 10:00 pm EST.

Real Estate

With his new-found success, the rewards this can bring and sometimes the problems, Drake has become extremely disciplined about handling his wealth. Taking financial advice, he has invested his money wisely in real estate; he is a silent partner in an Italian restaurant and owns numerous homes in Toronto, a bachelor pad in Miami and a luxury mansion in California.

In January 2011, Drake purchased a high-rise condo and the adjoining apartment for just under $2million at the Marquis Residences, on 1100 Biscayne Boulevard, in downtown Miami. The building is the tallest in Miami, with spectacular 360 degree views overlooking the bay. Drake had the suite refurbished and enlarged by knocking out a wall between the three bedroom 3,800 square foot suite and the 1,675 square foot apartment next door.

Drake eventually put the apartments back on the market in January 2012, less than a year after he had purchased the property. It was at the Marquis Residences that the video for DJ Khaled's, I'm On One, directed by Gil Green was filmed. The video – filmed during Memorial Day weekend 26-27 May 2012 – showed spectacular views overlooking the bay.

One of the more expensive homes Drake has acquired is a $7.7million Hollywood Hills mansion he bought in 2012. The seven-bedroom, nine-bathroom 7,500 sq. ft home features an abundance of amenities. Along with a 24-seat movie theatre, the pad also includes a gym, a wine cellar, recreational room, a mini spa and more. Drake's new home also has a massive swimming pool with waterfall accents and a cave, which is certainly sure to see quite a few parties in the future.

Future investment ambitions for Drake may include ownership of a vineyard, owing to his love of fine wines, and buying further properties around the world.

In July 2013, Drake placed one of his Toronto purchases up for sale. The Yorkville condo, situated on the twenty-second floor of a building on St Thomas Street, was put on the market for just over $4 million.

Record Deal

In June 2009, after the success of his mixtape So Far Gone, all the major record labels that had previously shunned him now came courting, which sparked one of the biggest bidding wars in rap history. Drake's management team, Hip Hop Since 1978 and Cortez Bryant – who also manage Lil Wayne – sealed the deal which is widely regarded as one of the most lucrative in the music industry. The deal, followed tough negotiations with executives from Universal Motown, Warner Music Group and Atlantic Records, in what Billboard magazine described as 'one of the biggest bidding wars ever.' The breakdown of the deal is as follows:

- Drake is signed with Aspire/Young Money/ Cash Money Records
- Drake's management negotiated a $2m advance and he retains all publishing rights to his songs. He will only pay 25 per cent of music sales revenues to the label as a 'distribution fee'
- He will be distributed by Universal Records.

The deal is a complete reversal of the usual record deals that new artists have imposed on them by the all-powerful record labels, with typical deals having the label owning 50 per cent of the masters and publishing rights. The majority of new artists sign financially restrictive '360 deals' that sap 50 per cent of tours, merchandising, film and TV revenues. These deals offer much more restrictive profit-sharing, with the artist usually only earning 10-20 per cent of all record sales.

Drake's management team certainly signed a great deal for their young protégé and he also cemented his partnership with Lil Wayne by staying with the Young Money crew. Drake's obvious mass appeal took effect as the labels fought for his signature. Shortly after signing the deal Drake dropped a freestyle entitled 9AM In Dallas. It sees Drake introspective and contemplating the expectations of the deal, with the imminent release of his debut album, Thank Me Later and wondering whether he can sell the records predicted of him.

Luckily his pessimism was unfounded and the album debuted at number one on the US Billboard 200 chart, with first week sales of 447,000.

Renaissance The

The Renaissance were formed in 2005 when Drake was 19, and consisted of fellow Torontonians, singers Melanie Fiona and Aion Clarke, aka Voyce Alexander with Dalton Tennant, aka D10 on piano/keyboard. The band played mainly popular songs of the day once a week in the basement of the Avocado Supper Club in downtown Toronto. Drake MC'd the evening, keeping the diners entertained and would sing along with Fiona and Clarke, with Drake also rapping a few verses over D10's keys. Drake remembers playing in the club while Rihanna was shooting the video for her debut single, Pon De Replay, directed by Little X (see **X Director**) with Kardinal Offishall making a cameo appearance in the video.

The end of The Renaissance came just before a possible tour of the United States, when Drake received a telephone call at home from the band's manager, informing him that he was out of the band and that in her words: 'I don't think music is your calling.' Drake was devastated and shocked but he has always stated that his time in the band and the way he was fired were good character building experiences. The band disbanded a month later.

After the band disbanded, Melanie Fiona went on to make a name for herself as an R&B singer. She has performed at the 2009 BET awards and has had numerous Grammy Award nominations. In 2012 she finally won two Grammy Awards for Best Traditional R&B Performance and Best R&B Song for her performance on Cee Lo Green's, Fool for You.

Dalton 'D10' Tennant still plays keyboards with Drake to this day and has been credited as producer on a number of Drake's songs. Dalton also introduced Drake to fellow producer Boi-1da in 2006, with Boi-1da going on to produce the smash hit, Best I Ever Had.

Aion Clarke has also gone on to have a successful music career as an R&B and soul performer and is signed to Warner Chapell Music. Clarke, who also doubles as a songwriter landed his first Billboard hit, Got Me Going by American R&B male group, Day 26. He also penned the single Dem Haters for pop princess Rihanna, from her platinum certified 2006 album, A Girl Like Me.

The band was briefly reunited on Sunday 20 February 2011, at the NBA All Star Entertainment Series weekend in Los Angeles. Over the weekend Melanie Fiona and Aion Clarke sang the Canadian National Anthem on consecutive nights, with Drake attending to perform the smash hit, What's My Name? with Rihanna during the half-time show.

Replacement Girl

Drake became the first unsigned Canadian rapper to have his music video featured on Black Entertainment Television, when his first single from the Comeback Season mixtape, Replacement Girl, was featured as the 'New Joint of the Day' on 30 April 2007. The music video, which featured Trey Songz, was directed by Shane Stirling and produced by fellow Canadians Boi-1da and Tyrone Williams, on the ATF label. Replacement Girl peaked at number twenty-one on the Bubbling Under R&B/Hip-Hop Single chart.

Remix Project

The Remix Project is a registered charity for the creative arts based in Toronto. Founded by Gavin Sheppard in 2006, Remix aims to help teenagers and young adults from disadvantaged homes in the city to fulfill their creative potential. Students at the centre can choose to study from a variety of courses including graphic design, photography, videography, engineering and production.

Most of Drake's ATF/OVO crew attended the centre at some stage, including Noah Shebib who ran the recording arts program, DJ Future the Prince who graduated from the business program – and is currently an ambassador for the centre – and Karla Moy – who ran 'All Things Fresh' Drake's first website and blog – who was a graduate of the creative arts program. Drake would often pay for studio recording time at the centre, funded by his Degrassi money and it was during one of these sessions that he met up with Shebib. Apparently some of the initial recordings for the So Far Gone mixtape where laid at the centre.

RIAA

The Recording Industry Association of America certification process is based on the number of albums and singles sold through all retail markets. The record label must make a request for certification from the RIAA and pay a fee to have the single or album sales audited.

The certification and numbers required to be sold are as follows:

- Gold: 500,000 sales
- Platinum: 1,000,000 sales
- Diamond: 10,000,000 sales

Up to and including October 2013, seventeen of Drake's songs have received certification by the RIAA, with him as the main artist, and these are listed below. His most successful singles to date have been the triple platinum certified, The Motto and Take Care with 3 million sales. Next best are Best I Ever Had and Started From the Bottom, with sales of over 2 million copies each. Drake has also featured on another thirteen songs that have been accredited by the RIAA but not as the main artist.

Three of which have been certified triple platinum, Rihanna's hit What's My Name? from her album Loud, DJ Khaled's I'm On One from his We the Best Forever and She Will, from Lil Wayne's album Tha Carter IV, all with sales of over 3 million. (see **Features**)

Drake's RIAA Certifications as Main Artist

Year	Single	Album	Certification
2009	Best I Ever Had	So Far Gone	Double Platinum
2009	Successful	So Far Gone	Gold
2009	I'm Goin' In	So Far Gone	Platinum
2010	Over	Thank Me Later	Gold
2010	Find Your Love	Thank Me Later	Platinum
2011	Miss Me	Thank me Later	Gold
2011	The Motto	Take Care	Triple Platinum
2011	Headlines	Take Care	Platinum
2011	Marvin's Room	Take Care	Gold
2011	Make Me Proud	Take Care	Platinum
2012	Take Care	Take Care	Triple Platinum
2012	HYFR	Take Care	Gold
2013	Started From The Bottom	Nothing Was The Same	Double Platinum
2013	Hold On We're Going Home	Nothing Was The Same	Platinum

Rider Demands

The backstage rider is presented to promoters by every touring act, and it contains detailed specifications on what the artist and his or her backstage crew require while they are at the venue. Drake's rider, which is presented by his tour manager Jamil Davis to the promoters, also deals with stage design, lighting and sound systems, the performer's dressing room requirements and all meals and drinks to be consumed on the premises.

While some of the demands may change due to the time of the year and the city he is performing in, Drake ensures that he and his backroom crew are well looked after. He stays true to his Jewish heritage and always demands a kosher catering menu. Other 2011-12 rider demands include:

- Entrée of either grilled or baked chicken
- Chicken wings
- Hot vegetarian dishes
- Assortment of pasta, ceasar salad, rice, bread rolls and potato salad
- 4 dozen natural scented incense sticks
- Bottles of Pinot Grigio wine
- Cases of Heineken
- Jack Daniels
- Bottles of Hennesy
- Cases of Grey Goose
- Dr Bronner peppermint soap
- E-Z Wider rolling papers
- Dutch Master Cigars

The rider may also include a little helpful reminder to the promoters in case they may need it, as in Drake's 2010 rider presented to the promoters reminding them that they 'should bring more subs and amps as hip-hop revolves around bass and volume.'

Right Above It

Drake featured on Right Above It, the first single from Lil Wayne's eighth studio album, I Am Not A Human Being, which was released in 2010. The track was recorded prior to Wayne's year-long prison sentence for weapon possession and was produced by Daniel 'Kane Beatz' Johnson. Johnson had also produced Bedrock, for the We Are Young Money album and Super Bass for Nicki Minaj's album, Pink Friday.

- Released: 17 August 2010
- Album: I Am Not A Human Being
- Label: Young Money, Cash Money, Universal Motown
- Length: 4:35
- Writers: Dwayne Carter Jr, Andrew Canton, Aubrey Graham, Daniel Johnson
- Producer: Daniel 'Kane Beatz' Johnson

The song was co-written by the producer Johnson, Drake, Wayne and Andrew Canton and was certified double platinum by the Recording Industry Association of America with sales of over 2 million copies, peaking at number six on the Billboard Hot 100 chart.

Rihanna

Barbadian singer-songwriter Robyn Rihanna Fenty released her debut album Music of the Sun, in 2005 on the Def Jam record label. She has worked with Drake on a number of tracks including the single Take Care, from Drake's second studio album of the same name. Drake originally wrote the song R.I.P. for Rihanna's fifth studio album, Loud, but the song didn't make the cut and was eventually recorded by the British singer-songwriter Rita Ora.

Drake has also featured on, and is credited as co-writer for Rihanna's hit single What's My Name? from her album Loud. The duo performed the song for the first time at the 53rd Grammy Awards on 13 February 2011. What's My Name? was nominated for the Best Rap/Sung Collaboration at the 2012 Grammy Awards and was certified double platinum by the Recording Industry Association of America.

The press around this time were suggesting that the pair were in a relationship, with both denying this saying that they were just good friends. However the rumours persisted, especially when Rihanna was photographed by the British press travelling on the underground train system to watch Drake perform at the London O2 arena in 2012, during his Club Paradise tour of Europe. Unfortunately for the celebrity watchers she was actually in London to publicise her first feature film *Battleships,* which debuted in the UK, on 11 April that year.

Rihanna has continued to produce smash hits and released her seventh studio album, Unapologetic in 2012, which spawned the hit singles Diamonds, Stay and Pour It Up.

R.I.P.

R.I.P. was originally intended for Rihanna's 2010 album, Loud and was co-written by Drake. After Rihanna decided not to run with the song, UK recording artist Rita Ora – who had heard Drake's original demo of the song – contacted him saying she wanted to record the song. Drake agreed and her recording of the song, which featured British rapper Tinie Tempah was an instant hit reaching number one in the UK charts upon its release. R.I.P. was Ora's first single from her debut album, ORA released on Jay Z's Roc Nation label.

- Released: 4 May 2012
- Album: ORA
- Label: Roc Nation Columbia
- Length: 3:49
- Writers: Aubrey Graham, Farhad Samadzada, Mikkel S Eriksen,Tor Erik Hermansen, Nneka Egbuna, Renee Wisdom, Saul Milton, Tinie Tempah, William Kennard
- Producer: Stargate Chase and Status
- Music Video: Emil Law

The music video for the single was directed by Emil Law and was shot in and around the East End of London, UK. As the support artist for Drake's Club Paradise tour, Ora performed R.I.P. as part of her set at the Manchester MEN arena on 1 April 2012.

Roberson Gee

Gee Roberson is the founder and co-CEO of the production and management company Hip Hop Since 1978, along with his partner Kyambo 'Hip-Hop' Joshua. Beginning his career as an intern at Jay Z's Roc-A-Fella Records in the early 1990s, he eventually rose to become senior Vice President of A&R and headed the label's urban music division. In 1998 he formed his own management company, Rock Da World, signing Kanye West as its first artist. Roberson had his big break when he worked on West's debut album, The College Dropout, which was released in 2004. The company changed its name to Hip Hop Since 1978 shortly afterwards.

In 2008, Roberson was instrumental in partnering HHS78 with Bryant Management and it was this partnership that enabled him to co-manage, Lil Wayne, Nicki Minaj, and Drake. He also helped to negotiate Drake's lucrative record deal in 2009. Roberson has also executive produced the top three selling rap albums in 2011: Wayne's Tha Carter IV, Jay Z and Kanye West's Watch the Throne and Drake's album Take Care.

In co-operation with Cortez Bryant, Roberson – who assumed the role of Geffen Records chairman in 2011 – developed a brand development and artist management powerhouse company called The Blueprint Group in 2012, with the aim of maximising the exposure of its artists in film, television and merchandise.

Rogers Communications

Rogers Communications Inc is a leading provider of wireless, digital cable TV, high speed internet and home phone services to consumers and businesses in Canada. Around the time Drake was corresponding with Lil Wayne, Drake's email address was drizzydrake@rogers.com and because of this email address, Wayne had mistakenly thought that Drake's real surname was Rogers. He often used it while name checking the Toronto rapper, with shout-outs of 'Drizzy Drake Rogers' in his songs and performances.

Room for Improvement

The self-financed Room for Improvement mixtape was released in February 2006 and was Drake's first official mixtape, uploading the mixtape onto his MySpace page as a free download. With 23 tracks, the mixtape was hosted by DJ Smallz from the Southern Smoke Series, who had a big reputation for introducing future stars. Featuring on the mixtape were Nickelus F, Trey Songz, Lupe Fiasco and Aion Clarke from Drake's old band The Renaissance Amir and Boi-1da produced the majority of the tracks on the mixtape.

Drake has stated that the music was decent, but being on his own at that time and without the backing of a major label the all important breakthrough was tough. 'What you tend to learn is this business is based on relationships and networking in a major way' he said. Drake borrowed money from his Uncle Larry Graham, the former Sly & the Family Stone guitarist and solo R&B star to help produce and record Room for Improvement and he made it available for free download from his MySpace page. The mixtape was re-released in 2009, featuring only 11 selected songs with no DJ and with a remix of Do What You Do.

- Released:14 February 2006
- Label: ATF
- Length: 68:00
- Producers: Matthew Samuels, Pharell Williams, Frank Dukes, AmiR, Dan Johnson

Ross 'Rozay' Rick

William Leonard Roberts II is better known as the American rapper Rick Ross. He was born in Coahoma County, Mississippi and raised in Miami, Florida adopting the stage name Rick Ross from a notorious Los Angeles drug trafficker. In a style that is similar to Drake's, with his 'Drizzy' moniker, Ross is also known by his own 'Rozay'. Ross shot to fame with his 2006 debut album Port of Miami, which was released through the Slip N Slide and Def Jam labels. The album reached number one on both the US Billboard 200 and R&B/Hip-Hop Album charts.

Drake first collaborated with Ross in 2010, on the single Aston Martin Music, from Ross' fourth studio album Teflon Don, which they both co-wrote. Since then the duo have collaborated on numerous songs including Pop That, Lord Knows, Diced Pineapples, Stay Schemin, DJ Khaled's triple platinum certified I'm On One and US, which featured a new verse from Drake. So far their collaborations have been well received, as evidenced by Lord Knows, from Take Care trending on Twitter on the day the album dropped. Ross has appeared at Drake's first three OVO Festival's held in Toronto.

Robert's led a very different lifestyle before entering the hip-hop world as Rick Ross. In the early 1990s he worked as a prison correctional officer in Florida, which he has said was an opportunity to 'wash my hands' after his best friend was sentenced to 10 years in prison for various alleged criminal misdemeanors.

Known for his explicit lyrics, alleged legal troubles and huge amount of tattoos, Ross founded the record label Maybach Music Group in 2009 and the label's first album was Ross' third studio album, Deeper Than Rap with Ross releasing his gold certified albums, Teflon Don and God Forgives I Don't, on the label. He is currently signed to the Def Jam record label.

Drake has said of Ross:

> 'He is one of my favourite people to work with and be around. One of the great things about being around Rozay is that he comes out with some great sayings, with some gems and when he talks to you about life, I'm wide eyed like a little kid. I just love making songs with him and I love to listen to what we have done together while driving around in the car.'

On 14 October 2011, Ross suffered two seizures within 24 hours and had to undergo tests in hospital to establish the cause. Ross' health problems have put their proposed collaboration on the album YOLO on the back burner until his health improves. They had been working together on the album at the time, exchanging verses and raps.

On 17 May 2012, Ross joined Drake on the Houston leg of his Club Paradise tour at the Toyota Center, along with French Montana, for the first live performance of their song Stay Schemin' from Ross' mixtape Rich Forever. Also in 2012 Ross was named the 'Hottest MC in the Game' by MTV beating Drake and fellow artists, Jay Z and Lil Wayne to the award. In April 2013, Ross along with Drake and Lil Wayne joined DJ Khaled on the single No New Friends, the lead single from his seventh studio album Suffering From Success, reprising the crew from the triple platinum single I'm On One. His sixth studio album, Mastermind is due for release early in 2014.

S

Saturday Night Live

Drake first appeared on the popular American show *Saturday Night Live* on 15 October 2011. He performed Headlines, and then fellow Young Money star Nicki Minaj joined him on stage as the duo performed their hit Make Me Proud, the second single from his album Take Care.

Later in the show Drake took part in a series of short comedy sketches and interviews with host Andy Samber. One sketch looked at his obsession with sweaters – Drake allegedly has over 500 – with both wearing identical sweaters during the hilarious interview. Later on 'Weekend Update' Drake dressed as a werewolf rapping about stealing little children's Halloween candy. Most reviews of the show were favourable and agreed that Drake had been a popular guest, with a great sense of humour while taking part in the sketches.

Search The

Drake originally planned to call his debut studio album The Search, but then decided to call the album Thank Me Later.

Shebib Noah

Drake's closest friend and producer, Noah '40' Shebib was born in Toronto in 1983 and grew up in a family steeped in the entertainment industry. His father is the acclaimed director Donald Shebib, who directed the cult 1970 Canadian feature Going Down the Road, so it was perhaps inevitable that he would become involved in the entertainment industry.

He became a child acting prodigy, starring in the TV series *Goosebumps*, *The Mighty Jungle* and also the cult movie, *The Virgin Suicides*.

During his acting career Shebib decided that he didn't like the limelight in front of the cameras and preferred to be behind the screen. Ever since that time he has leaned towards the technical side of the entertainment industry, preferring others to be in the limelight. He began his interest in the music industry when he used the money he had made from his early acting career, to buy a four-track tape deck and sampler, making music in the basement of the family home. By the age of 12 he had become competent with most computer programs and had started DJ'ing for family and friend's parties under the name, DJ Decibel. This hobby brought him into contact with different music genres such as hip-hop and rap and served as a great apprenticeship for his future career.

When Shebib was 20 he began an internship with Noel 'Gadget' Campbell, a well-known music mixer from Toronto, who has become a mentor and the duo continue to work together to this day.

Shebib earned his nickname '40' while he was working as an engineer with Campbell's Blacksmith Entertainment label when he was 21. Payback and Illy, from Toronto rap group G Squad happened to be in the same studio while Shebib was working on tracks laid down by the rapper Jellestone and the R&B singer Divine Brown. They were amazed that he was working behind his console when they left the studio and on their return to the studio the next day he was still in position working, apparently without having had a break or sleeping. So they nicknamed him 40 days and 40 nights.

The Jellestone and Brown records were Shebib's first major label recordings which put him on the map, especially Brown's first single, Old Skool from her debut 2005 album Divine Brown, which was an R&B hit and certified gold in Canada.

177

Shebib met Drake for the first time – after being introduced by a mutual friend – on the set of the Replacement Girl music video in 2007, where he played Drake a number of beats. Although Drake didn't buy any of the beats that day, he did agree to buy a couple of days studio time at the Remix Project where Shebib worked and after being suitably impressed with what he heard, Shebib became Drake's engineer and musical director for his live shows. Through the following months of trial and error, he saw how frustrated Drake was becoming in trying to identify his sound with different producers, until he finally recognised what Drake was searching for and decided to produce him himself. The duo eventually produced their first track, Brand New, with the beat written by Dalton 'D10' Tennant with Shebib and Tennant sharing production duties.

Shebib has said of his first meeting with Drake, that he had initially started off working in the studio for 2 days as a hired engineer and by the third day he and Drake had agreed to take over the world. The duo had a lot in common due to their mutual love of R&B, they had both been child actors and had also dropped out of school at an early age to pursue a career in the music industry. Shebib cites fellow Toronto producers like Gadget, Saukrates, Kardinal Offishall and Mazzaman as his inspirations.

Drake has said of his friend and producer:

> 'He's worked with me every single night I've set foot inside the studio since Comeback Season. He knows what I'm capable of and he's not afraid to say 'You can do better than that, or you can write a better verse, or that's it were done!'

Drake calls Shebib his 'right hand' on the opening track from his Comeback Season mixtape, The Presentation and pays further tribute to '40' on the credit sleeve of his Thank Me Later album.

Noah Shebib has won numerous individual awards during his music career. On 29 June 2012 he won the Songwriter of the Year Award, from The American Society of Composers, Authors and Publishers (ASCAP). The award honours the most performed songs on the R&B/Hip-Hop and Rap charts, with Shebib winning the award for penning four of the most performed songs. The songs included two which featured Drake; Jamie Foxx's, Fall for Your Type and I'm On One, by DJ Khaled and Drake's own singles Headlines and Marvin's Room.

Shebib was also nominated at the 2012 Juno Awards for the Producer of The Year Award.

When he was 22, Shebib was diagnosed with multiple sclerosis (MS); his mother Tedde Moore was also diagnosed with MS 2 years later, although the disease is not hereditary. The early diagnosis of MS has obviously shaped Shebib's life, but he tries to not let it interfere with his work. He is an active campaigner for the National MS Society and in March 2013 participated in the campaign for MS awareness week, with messages and information about MS beamed across three mega-electronic billboards in Times Square New York.

Noah Shebib is currently managed by Hip Hop Since 1978.

Sher

Sher is Drake's mother's maiden name. (see **Mother**).

She Will

She Will – originally intended to be called Maybe She Will – is a song by American rapper Lil Wayne, which featured a verse by Drake and was the fourth single from Wayne's album, Tha Carter IV. It was intended to include a verse from Rick Ross on the track, but that verse never made the final cut.

The single reached number one on the US Billboard Hot R&B/Hip-Hop Song chart and was certified triple platinum by the Recording Industry Association of America, with sales of over 3 million on 28 October 2011.

- Released: 16 August 2011
- Album: Tha Carter IV
- Label: Young Money, Cash Money, Universal Republic
- Length: 5:07
- Writers: Dwayne Carter Jr, Aubrey Graham, Tyler Williams
- Producer: T-Minus
- Music Video: DJ Scoop Doo

She Will was produced by Drake's longtime associate from his Replacement Girl days, Tyler 'T-Minus' Williams who is also credited with co-writing the track. The music video was directed by DJ Scoop Doo, a regular collaborator with Wayne. He had filmed The Nino Brown Story a 2008 documentary about Lil Wayne. The DVD follows Wayne performing live on tour, bowling with friends and behind the scenes footage of Wayne and guests in the recording studio.

Slack Terral

Terral 'Hollaback' Slack managed Drake from shortly after the release of Drake's first mixtape – the 2006 DJ Smallz hosted – Room for Improvement. After hearing his music, Slack decided to use his extensive list of contacts and approached various artists and producers to collaborate with Drake, which resulted in the breakthrough 2007 mixtape Comeback Season. (see **Comeback Season**)

Drake released Replacement Girl, featuring Trey Songz on 30 April as the first single from the mixtape, with Slack executive producing the music video, which featured on BET. Managing Drake through his artist and booking company, Bigger Picture Entertainment, Slack also introduced his young protégé to a sustained marketing campaign, which resulted in Drake being interviewed on radio, featuring in various magazine publications and increasing his social network presence via MySpace. It was the interest resulting in the release of the Comeback Season mixtape and the sustained marketing campaign that propelled the young Canadian rapper to be the hottest unsigned MC and had the record labels finally sitting up and taking notice.

Slaight Allan

Allan Slaight, has been involved in the Canadian Broadcasting industry for over five decades, with his ideas and business acumen leading him to become one of Canada's most successful philanthropists.

Starting as a news reporter in 1948 with interests in music, television and radio, his company Slaight Communications was formed in 1985 from the ashes of Slaight Broadcasting, which he formed in 1971. He would soon go on to purchase Standard Broadcasting Corporation Ltd, which would become Canada's biggest privately owned multimedia company.

Canada's Walk of Fame named an award after Allan Slaight in recognition of his contribution to Canadian society and his charity work through the Slaight Foundation. In 2013 he and his wife Emmanuelle Gattuso announced a $50 million donation to Canada's Princess Margaret Cancer Hospital from the foundation, after the hospital had cared for her as she successfully underwent treatment for breast cancer.

Drake won only the second ever Allan Slaight Award in 2011 which aims to honour young Canadians who make a positive impact in the fields of music, film, literature, visual or performing arts, sports, innovation or philanthropy. Drake received the award during Canada's Walk of Fame Awards show on 1 October. The award came with a $10,000 charitable donation, which Drake presented to Dixon Hall, a Toronto-based community group, whose aim is to bring greater opportunities for the low-income neighborhoods of Toronto. The CEO of Slaight Communications, Gary Slaight called Drake 'a true Canadian ambassador who continues to prove that with hard work, dreams can become reality.'

Drake joins jazz singer Nikki Yanofsky and two-time Grammy Award winning R&B artist and friend Melanie Fiona as winners of the award to date.

Smith Courtne

Courtne Smith is a long-time friend of Drake from Toronto and is an original member of the All Things Fresh crew. She has been with Drake since he started out on his music career and she was his personal assistant for over 3 years. One of her early memories of Drake is of him singing to her with one of the first songs he had written. Due to his being worried about her reaction to his singing and the song lyrics, he had told her it had been written by somebody else, but his mother gave the game away and told her that Drake had actually written the song, much to Drake's embarrassment.

After years of following Drake around the world as his PA, Smith decided she needed to branch out on her own and in October 2011, launched her first business venture called Queen Shmink. The company is Smith's platform to create and advertise her own personal style and taste on the fashion world.

So Far Gone EP

After signing his record deal, the So Far Gone (SFG) mixtape was slimmed down into an Extended Play (EP) for sale, and it became the fifth best-selling rap album of 2009, despite the fact that all the material, bar two songs had been available for free on the original mixtape. Released as a result of the success of the SFG mixtape, the extended play version was released on 15 September 2009 and had seven tracks in total, five from the mixtape and two new tracks, I'm Going In and The Fear. Featuring on the EP were Lil Wayne, Trey Songz, Bun B and Young Jeezy.

The last track on the EP was called Fear, with Drake explaining that it would be the link between the EP and his debut studio album, Thank Me Later. The last line of the last verse on the track Fear would also be the first line of the first track Fireworks, on the Thank Me Later album.

- Released: 15 September 2009
- Extended Play (EP)
- Label: Young Money, Cash Money Universal Motown
- Length: 33:50
- Writers: Aubrey Graham, Noah Shebib
- Producers: Noah Shebib, Arthur McArthur, Kesown Cassel, Matthew Samuels, DJ Khalil

The EP hit number one on the US Billboard Top Rap Album chart and won the Rap Recording of The Year at the 2010 Juno Awards.

In July 2010, with sales of over 500,000, the EP was certified gold by the Recording Industry Association of America. Three singles off the EP were also certified by the RIAA: the platinum certified singles, Best I Ever Had and I'm Goin' In, with over 1 million sales and the gold certified Successful, with over 500,000 sales.

So Far Gone Mixtape

Drake's third official mixtape So Far Gone, was released onto his October's Very Own Label on 13 February 2009. The mixtape had 18 tracks and sees Drake drifting effortlessly from rapping to singing. Two tracks were released as future singles: Successful, featuring Trey Songz and the hit single Best I Ever Had.

The mixtape, produced by fellow Canadians, Noah Shebib, Boi-1da and 'T Minus', received critical acclaim from both professional critics and fans alike, with MTV making it the hottest mixtape of 2009. The majority of the tracks were mixed and mastered in room 718 at the Beverley Wiltshire Hotel, Los Angeles, over a week in January 2009 – Drake and Shebib were in LA with Lil Wayne, who was attending the Grammy Awards ceremony – with the rest laid down in Shebib's high-rise Toronto condo at 1503 Fort Boulevard Apartments.

Drake has said that he had wanted the music on the mixtape to also have an R&B sound, so he enlisted the help of R&B singers Lloyd, Trey Songz and Omarion to provide guest vocals, with Lil Wayne also featuring on four tracks. The mixtape was available to download from October's Very Own blog, and went on to be downloaded over 30 million times.

On 22 February 2009, a release party for the mixtape was held at the 6 Degrees nightclub in Toronto hosted by NBA basketball legend and friend LeBron James with American model Bria Myles and James' fellow Miami Heat basketball player Chris Bosh also in attendance.

Talking about the making of the mixtape, Drake said that he and his family were in a dark place when he made So Far Gone, with lots of yelling and crying at home. The song, The Calm is a case in point and was written at '40's high-rise condo at 1503 Fort Boulevard Apartments on one crazy night. Drake had arrived at the apartment with over $1,000 worth of champagne with '40' giving him a hard time because they were so broke at the time. Drake then had a blazing row with his uncle over the telephone, with '40' saying he has never seen Drake so distraught or emotionally beat up. After the row with his uncle, Drake tells '40' he wanted to put some music down and 5 hours later the track, The Calm was finished.

With the mixtape completed, Drake decided to use MySpace to give the music away free to his fans and to let them decide if they liked it or not, Drake explained to Complex magazine that the mixtape is a story of his life at that time:

> 'Starting in January 2008 when I was confused, I gave up acting to do this music thing. I was also in a destructive relationship with a female and I was just in a bad space. It starts with this monologue, Lust for Life of me crying out. Then it goes to Housatlantavegas, which is about what I felt about the girl I was with at that time. I just felt nothing was ever good enough for her. Then we move to Successful with all the dreams that that held. We then moved onto Let's Call It Off, which is the breakup of our relationship. Coincidentally when I broke up with that girl, a week later I went to Houston and met Lil Wayne and that's where November 18th comes from.'

He went on:

> 'Best I Ever Had is about a wonderful girl from Toronto who represented everything I love about the city. She changed my life for the better and helped me make music about real life, with each song being like a time marker of my life.'

- Released: 13 February 2009
- Mixtape
- Label: October's Very Own
- Length: 70:35
- Writers: Aubrey Graham, Noah Shebib
- Producers: Noah Shebib, Kanye West , DJ Screw Dalton Tennent, Arthur McArthur, Kesown Cassel, MegaMan, Matthew Samuels

So Far Gone Tour

The So Far Gone tour started at the Purchase Arena, New York, on 17 April 2009 and finished back in New York at the famous SOB Club where Drake played the Hot 97 Who's Next show, on 26 May 2009. The tour sold out nearly every night with Noah Shebib acting as production/stage manager and playing keyboards. Trey Songz made a guest appearance on the Atlanta leg of the tour, joining Drake on stage to perform their hit single Successful.

So Far Gone Tour Venues:

April
04-17: New York, NY. Purchase College Purchase
04-18: New York, NY. Daemen College Elmhurst
04-22: Florida, FL. O'Connell Center University
04-24: Columbus, OH. Club Ice
04-25: Bowling Green, OH. Bowling Green University
04-30: Newark, DW. Bob Carpenter Center

May
05-01: Statesboro, GA. Georgia Southern Performing Arts
05-02: Atlanta, GO. The Loft
05-09: New Orleans, LO. McAllister Center
05-13: Toronto, ON. Sound Academy
05-15: Chicago, IL. House of Blues
05-22: San Bernadino, CA.Santos Manuel Student Union
05-23: Los Angeles, CA. Luckman Fine Arts Complex
05-26: New York, NY.SOB Club New York

Songz Trey

Tremaine 'Trey Songz' Neverson is an American singer-songwriter, rapper, record producer and actor from Virginia, US. Discovered by record producer Troy Taylor after winning a talent show in 2000, Songz signed to Atlantic Records in 2002 and released his debut album, I Gotta' Make It in 2005. He featured on Drake's first music video for the single Replacement Girl, from his second mixtape Comeback Season, with the video featuring on Black Entertainment Television as the 'New Joint of the Day' on 30 April 2007. Drake had previously appeared in a cameo role in the music video for the Trey Songz single, Wonder Woman earlier the same year.

The pair met after Drake had sent a demo of his song Replacement Girl to Songz, who listened to it, liked it and he has said of that first contact, 'I don't just jump on any feature, I turn down a lot of things people send to me, as they are not up to par, but after hearing this I was in.' It was Songz who sang the chorus and came up with the hook on Successful, one of Drake's breakthrough hits. The duo linked up once again on the track, Unusual from Songz's gold certified album Passion, Pain & Pleasure which was released in September 2010.

Sotto Sotto

Sotto Sotto, located on Avenue Road is one of Drake's favourite Italian restaurants in Toronto. When he is back in Toronto and visiting Sotto Sotto, he has his favourite waiter Angelo bring over a tray of shots and appetisers for him and his friends, while he chills at his favourite table, under the restaurant's low slung alcove. The restaurant is name checked on the tracks, 5AM In Toronto and also on Pound Cake/Paris Morton Music 2 featuring Jay Z from Drake's 2013 album, Nothing Was the Same.

Started From the Bottom

Released on 6 February 2013, Started From the Bottom is the first single from Drake's third studio album, Nothing Was the Same. The single peaked at number two on both the US Hot R&B/Hip-Hop Song and the US Rap Song charts giving Drake his 30th top ten hit on the Billboard R&B /Hip-Hop chart since his first – Best I Ever Had – in 2009.

- Released: 6 February 2013
- Album: Nothing Was The Same
- Label: Young Money, Cash Money, Universal Republic
- Length: 2:53
- Writers: Aubrey Graham, Noah Shebib, Michael Coleman
- Producer: Mike Zombie
- Music Video: Director X

The music video was directed by Director X and won the MuchMusic Hip-Hop Video of The Year Award in 2013, with Drake's mother making a cameo appearance in the video. Started From the Bottom was certified double platinum with sales of over 2 million on 23 August 2013.

Successful

Successful is the second single off Drake's, So Far Gone EP and was released on the same day as his other hit single, Best I Ever Had. Written by Drake, Trey Songz, Lil Wayne and producer Noah Shebib, the song, which also featured on the So Far Gone mixtape, was certified Gold by the RIAA with sales of over 500,000. Songz, who also featured on the track, remembered the first time he heard the song after Drake had emailed him with the words 'let me know what you think.' Songz remembers:

> 'He sent me this track one night and I was in the studio. It was simplistic, eerie and dark, and I couldn't think what I wanted to hear on it, so I did a whole bunch of harmonies. I knew I had something.'

- Released: 13 February 2009
- Album: So Far Gone EP
- Label: Young Money, Cash Money, Universal Motown
- Length: 5:51
- Writers: Aubrey Graham, Noah Shebib, Dwayne Carter, Tremaine Neverson
- Producer: Noah Shebib
- Music Video: Chris White

The music video for the song was filmed in Toronto and was directed by Chris White, winning both the Video of The Year and Cinematographer of The Year awards at the 2010 MuchVIBE Hip Hop Award ceremony. The video shows Drake and Songz together on a high rise balcony with the Toronto night skyline as the background and ending with an inspirational quote from US President Barack Obama. Successful, which also featured Lil Wayne on verse four, was released on 13 February 2009 and reached number two on the US Rap Song and number three on the Hot R&B/Hip-Hop Song charts, becoming Trey Songz third Top 20 hit.

T

Take Care

Take Care is Drake's second studio album and was released on 15 November 2011, later than the original release date of Drake's birthday 24 October, due to sample clearance problems. The album debuted at number one on the US Billboard 200, Rap Album and R&B/Hip-Hop Album charts, with first week sales of 631,000. On 31 January 2012, the album was certified platinum by the Recording Industry Associates of America, with sales of over 1 million copies in the United States before going double platinum with sales of over 2 million in July 2013.

Drake has said that he came up with the title for the album while he was on the tour bus in Birmingham, England going to a show. He says:

> 'We always used the phrase 'take care' in passing conversation and I really took so much care making the album, I just knew I was going to be attentive, clear and be totally immersed in the making of this project. So Take Care really worked as a title. Thank Me Later felt weird making an album for sale within four months on a tour bus, and I just felt we rushed it. So I really wanted to produce something special.'

With songs on the album featuring Rihanna, Nicki Ninaj, Rick Ross and Lil Wayne, Take Care peaked at number five on the UK Album Chart and on 16 December 2011, was certified gold with the British Recorded Music Industry for sales of over 100,000 copies.

XO crew member and fellow Canadian 'Dropxlife' is credited for designing the artwork for the album cover, which shows Drake seated at a table surrounded by opulence but looking unhappy. Drake has said he wanted to express the feeling that 'here's this 24 year-old guy with a great apartment, filled with every trinket, plenty of money, but when I am by myself I am lonely.' The cover was photographed at Joso's restaurant in Toronto.

- Released: 15 November 2011
- Album: Take Care
- Label: Young Money, Cash Money, Universal Republic
- Length: 79:49
- Writers: Aubrey Graham, Noah Shebib, Samuel Matthews, Tyler Williams, Abel Tesfaye
- Producers: Noah Shebib, Boi-1da, T-Minus Williams, Abel Tesfaye, Doc Mc Kinney, Jamie X, Aubrey Graham

Singles from the Take Care Album

Title	Featuring	Release date
Marvin's Room: promotional single		28 June 2011
Headlines		31 July 2011
Make Me Proud	Nicki Minaj	13 October 2011
The Motto	Lil Wayne	29 November 2011
Take Care	Rihanna	21 February 2012
HYFR	Lil Wayne	24 March 2012

Drake eventually released six singles from the album, with The Motto becoming the most successful single with sales of over 3 million copies in the US, his first single to reach that milestone. Most of the album was recorded at the Metalworks Studio Toronto. On 20 February 2013, Take Care won Drake his first Grammy Award for Best Rap Album.

Tattoos

Drake has a number of tattoos on his body:

- The words 'ALL KINDS' are written on the inside of his right arm. 'All Kinds' was the name of a track that didn't make the Take Care album.
- The Toronto CN tower – on the inside of his left arm

Drake who has made no secret of his respect for the late Grammy Award nominated R&B singer Aaliyah, has had a second tattoo paying homage to both her and his home city of Toronto. He posted a picture on his Twitter account showing himself getting inked with 416 – the area code of Toronto – down the right side of his body, with the number 4 only partially shaded so that the number 1 looks more prominent. Aaliyah's birthday is January 16 or 116, which the tattoo clearly shows. He showed off the tattoo for the first time in public to the crowd at the 3rd OVO Festival in Toronto to rapturous applause.

On his back Drake has the following tattoos;

- The OVO owl just below his right shoulder
- Aaliyah's image on the left side of his back
- A flying angel on his left shoulder
- The phrase 'If I died today, it'll be a holiday' on his right shoulder, followed by the words:

  - atf (All Things Fresh)
  - ovo (Octobers Very Own)
  - ymcmb (Young Money Cash Money)
  - reps up

In 2013 Drake added two portraiture tattoos of his recently deceased grandmother and uncle in their younger days onto his back.

Thank Me Later

While performing at the University of Missouri in Kansas City during his Away From Home tour, Drake revealed that he would be submitting the final copy of his highly anticipated debut album, Thank Me Later. On Monday 26 April he told the assembled audience that the show would go down in history, not only because it was his first time in Kansas City, but that it would be the city where the final cut of his album would be turned in.

In February 2010, Drake told *Rolling Stone* Magazine about the problems in trying to finally complete the album. He and his producers, Boi-1da and Noah Shebib, had travelled to Jamaica in order to finish the album with an array of talent reaching out to contribute. But Drake soon discovered that having a wealth of star power at his disposal wasn't necessarily what he needed. He said:

> 'You realise sometimes, you sit with all the producers that you thought would make the change for you, you go to a bunch of places that you thought would be inspiring, but sometimes you realise that simple stuff when it was easy and carefree, you realise that's where you need to get back to.'

Thank Me Later was originally planned for a March release but finally dropped on 15 June 2010. The entire album leaked on 1 June before its official release date, but Drake remained philosophical about it saying he has given free music away for years and he's good about it and looking forward to the 15 June. He needn't have worried, with first-week sales of 447,000 copies the album debuted at number one on the US Billboard 200, Billboard's R&B/Hip-Hop Album and Rap Album charts.

On 20 July 2010, the album was certified platinum by the Recording Industry Association of America with sales of over 1 million copies and has sold over 1,500,000 copies in the US to date.

- Released: 15 June 2010
- Album: Thank Me Later
- Label: Young Money, Cash Money, Universal Motown
- Length: 61:02
- Writers: Graham, Shebib, Samuels, West, Carter
- Producers: Noah Shebib, Boi-1da, Francis & The Lights, Swizz Beatz, Timbaland, Kanye West

Singles from the Thank Me Later Album

Title	Featuring	Release date
Over		8 March 2010
Find Your Love		5 May 2010
Miss Me	Lil Wayne	1 June 2010
Fancy	T.I & Swizz Beatz	3 August 2010

Explaining the title for the album Drake stated that on the first play people may not get the music or the concept for the album, but after further plays they would and eventually thank him later for it. He had also made a deliberate decision to add singing to the mix, undertaking intensive vocal training while making the album with vocal coach Dionne Osborne.

As part of the publicity surrounding the album's release, a crowd of more than 25,000 fans had gathered at South Street Seaport's Pier 17 in Lower Manhattan, to see Drake on the day before his long-awaited debut album, Thank Me Later was finally released.

Unfortunately, he never managed to perform for his fans as the police decided the crowd, being more than three times the numbers expected and who were being managed by limited security, were becoming too unruly and they stopped the performance. When it became clear that Drake would not be performing, fans began hurling bottles and metallic lawn chairs. Fighting broke out and fearing a riot, the police sprayed mace to disperse the crowd.

The album's cover artwork was designed by Toronto graphic designer Darkie Made, who had also designed the original cover for the Best I Ever Had single, before it was deemed too obscure by iTunes.

Thank Me Later/Virgin America

Upon touchdown at Toronto Pearson International Airport on 29 June 2010, Drake gave the thumbs up to the assembled crowds in front of the Virgin Airbus A320 'Air Drake'. He had travelled from San Francisco International Airport to promote the launch of Virgin America's new Toronto service. The plane, emblazoned with the artwork from his Thank Me Later album, was greeted by a water cannon salute, an international welcoming committee and a red carpet party of dignitaries on the arrival tarmac. (see **Photographs**)

Virgin Group founder Sir Richard Branson, flight guests, industry leaders, fellow Torontonians and VIPs then joined Drizzy for a cocktail party held at The Thompson Hotel rooftop bar. Later that evening Drake's DJ – Future the Prince – entertained the guests in the hotel's nightclub spinning beats into the early hours.

The Motto

MuchVIBE Hip-Hop Video of the Year 2012

The Motto is a digital iTunes Store bonus track from Drake's second studio album Take Care and features Lil Wayne and Tyga. Peaking at number one on the US Rap Song and number four on the R&B/Hip-Hop Song charts, The Motto was the second and most successful single from the Take Care album. In April 2013 the single achieved triple platinum status in the US, selling over 3 million copies and was nominated for Best Rap Song at the 2013 Grammy Awards.

- Released: 29 November 2011
- Album: Take Care
- Label: Young Money, Cash Money, Universal Republic
- Length: 3:07
- Writers: Karmanaut, Dwayne Carter Jr, N Cobey, Tyler Williams, Salvatore Conto
- Producer: T-Minus
- Music Video: Hyghly Alleyne, Lamar Taylor

The music video, shot on 35mm film in Oakland, California on November 2011 was released onto Vimeo on 21 December 2011. Directed by Hyghly Alleyne and Lamar Taylor, the video features Lil Wayne and Tyga, and opens with a message from Wanda Salvatto, the mother of Mac Dre, a Bay area rapper who was shot and killed in 2004. The video starts off with Salvatto looking into the camera and addressing her son directly. As the song progresses, the clip includes shots of Oakland and San Francisco. Drake is filmed mostly by a camera from the passenger seat of his car, as he cruises around the Bay area, rapping the motto YOLO, 'You Only Live Once'. The video was the winner of the 2012 MuchVIBE Hip-Hop Video of the year, with Hyghly Alleyne accepting the award on behalf of Drake and his partner Lamar Taylor.

The N Soundtrack

The N Soundtrack album, released in August 2006 for the American television channel 'The N' featured songs from TV shows which were airing at the time in North America. The album had eleven tracks including contributions from *Degrassi: The Next Generation, Beyond the Break, South of Nowhere, Instant Star* and *Whistler*. Released on Nick Records the album was particularly notable for containing the first recording made by Drake with Do What You Do for sale. The whole album was produced by Boi-1da.

Do What You Do also appeared on Drake's first mixtape Room for Improvement and remixed on the Comeback Season mixtape, featuring Malice and Nickelus F.

The One

- Released: 21 July 2009
- Album: Stronger With Each Tear
- Label: Geffen Records
- Length: 3:29
- Writers: Mary J Blige, Aubrey Graham, Esther Dean, Rodney Jerkins, Tyler Williams, Salvatore Conto
- Producer: Rodney 'Darkchild' Jerkins
- Music Video: Anthony Mandler

The One is the first single from Mary J. Blige's album Stronger with Each Tear, produced by Rodney Jerkins aka Darkchild and written by Blige, Drake – who also features on the single – Esther Dean and Rodney Jerkins.

The music video was directed by Anthony Mandler and featured Drake, although he had just reinjured his knee during the America's Most Wanted tour days before. The single failed to make an impact and debuted at number 63 on the Billboard Hot 100.

Toronto

Drake was born on 24 October 1986 in Toronto, Ontario which is the largest city in Canada, with over 2.7 million citizens. The city is sometimes nicknamed T.O. or T-Dot and is one of the most cosmopolitan cities in the world. Drake has said of his hometown, which he reps at every opportunity:

> 'Toronto is the biggest inspiration behind my music, everything I do, I do for Toronto. It's a city I really believe in, it's got a great bunch of people and we've got a lot of undiscovered things in Toronto. We got great looking women, nightlife, restaurants, clubs and talent. First I just wanna' bring the city to the forefront. I feel like every place needs an ambassador. Each city needs somebody to show the rest of the world how magic that place can be. I think Jay Z does it great for New York, a lot of people do it for Atlanta and Kanye does it for Chicago. A lot of rappers take it upon themselves to rep their city so I just wanna' be that guy for Toronto.'

Since the inaugural event in 2010, Drake holds his annual OVO Festival at the Molson Ampitheatre in Toronto during the Civic two-day holiday. Notable performers at the festival have included Jay Z, Eminem, Stevie Wonder and Lil Wayne.

Tours

As Headline Artist:

Away From Home 2010
Light Dreams & Nightmares 2010
Club Paradise 2012
Would You Like A Tour? 2013-14

As Featured Guest Artist:

America's Most Wanted 2009

Twitter

Drake has over 13.5 million followers on Twitter and he tweets whenever time allows, with a total of 1,501 tweets as of 1December. His Twitter handle is @drake and he has also used @drakkardnoir, following 629 at present.

Tyga

Michael Stevenson aka Tyga, is an American rapper from Compton, California. He started his career in the music industry by recording and promoting his own mixtapes, which brought him to the attention of Gym Class Heroes member Travie McCoy, who signed him to his Bad Squad Label. He appeared on the remix to Fall Out Boy's single, Arms Race for the label, which also featured Kanye West and Lil Wayne performing the hit on MTV's video music awards in 2007. He has continued to work with Wayne, signing to Young Money/Universal Republic Records label in 2007.

Being a part of Young Money Entertainment, Tyga joined Drake on the America's Most Wanted Tour and since then the pair have collaborated on a number of projects. They were both part of the 2009 We Are Young Money compilation album and Tyga joined Drake on his 2010 Light Dreams and Nightmares tour, replacing Clipse as the opening act. Tyga also featured on the triple platinum selling track, The Motto from Drake's album Take Care, which also featured Lil Wayne. Drake has returned the favour, featuring on Tyga's second album Careless World: Rise of the Last King, which reached number one on both the US Rap and R&B charts in 2012.

Tyga won a Grammy Award for Best Rap/Sung Collaboration for Deuces with Chris Brown & Kevin McCall in 2011.

U

Uncle Steve

Steve Sher is the brother of Sandi Graham, and Drake's relationship with his uncle has been a regular theme on a lot of his material. The two have an extremely close bond and he is more of a father figure due to the absence of Drake's natural father for most of his early life. Drake credits his uncle with moulding him into the man he is today.

Drake has expressed much of his personal experiences in his lyrics, with his upbringing and family being two of the main themes. His uncle is a huge part of Drake's life, with the second verse on the song, Look What You've Done being a tribute. In one of Drake's unreleased songs entitled The Winner, he once again praises his uncle as his hero who looked after the family. The sleeve notes of Drake's second album Take Care, contained a lot of messages of thanks to the people that have supported him and included a tribute to his Uncle Steve.

While receiving his award for Songwriter of the Year at the BMI Urban Awards in 2011, he again spoke about his uncle saying:

> 'And to my uncle who sat me down after the President of one of the major record labels told me that I didn't have what it took to make it in the music industry, he encouraged me and told me that I should keep going, as I have something special.'

His Uncle Steve was also present at the Jarvis Collegiate Institute in Toronto to see Drake receiving his diploma after graduating in August 2012, with Drake praising him for his guidance and support throughout his teenage years. Drake has also tweeted a picture of himself as a small child with his uncle stating simply on the caption: 'Without this man there is no me...Uncle Steve.'

On 10 February 2013, at the Staples Center in LA, Steve Sher stood proudly alongside his nephew being interviewed on the red carpet prior to Drake receiving his Grammy Award for Best Rap Album for Take Care.

Underground Kings

Underground Kings, is a track off Drake's album Take Care, which pays homage to American rapper Yo Gotti. Drake watched Gotti record in the studio in Memphis, Tennessee while visiting his father who lived in the city. In the lyrics he acknowledges his connection with the southern city due to his father's family and how he sat in the studio watching Gotti record, learning how it was done, what the guys were wearing and how they carried themselves. Drake has also acknowledged that just being around Gotti and the musicians in the studio shaped a lot of his early memories and his decision to make a career in the music industry.

Unit 5

Unit 5 at 163 Sterling Road was owned by Noah Shebib, and it was here that the duo laid down some of the tracks off Drake's two mixtapes, Comeback Season and So Far Gone. Situated in Bloordale Village Toronto, the original building consisted of a number of small rooms, one of which Shebib converted into a music studio. The premises have now been taken over by The Sterling Theatre and Film Society.

V

Vaughan Road Academy

Situated in the Oakwood-Vaughan neighbourhood of Ontario, Vaughan Road High School caters for students from age 14-18 (grades 9-12). The school founded in 1927, was the first high school built in the Borough of York.

Drake attended the school after leaving Forest Hill Collegiate Institute but dropped out to concentrate on his role as Jimmy Brooks on the TV series, *Degrassi: The Next Generation* and to provide money to help support the family finances as his mother was unable to work, due to a chronic illness.

Drake later went on to complete his High School Diploma in 2012, working with Vaughan Road teacher Kim Janzen for 5 months, eventually graduating with a score of 97 per cent in his final exam and an overall score of 88 per cent for the course. (see **Diploma**)

Vivoli

Vivoli is an Italian restaurant situated on College Street, at the heart of Little Italy, Toronto. Drake frequents the restaurant whenever he is in town and the manager Mario always ensures he gets his favourite table in the corner. Drake has said: 'Every time I come home, when the city gets too crazy I just go to Vivoli and invite all my friends, we drink, eat and have fun. That's one of my favourite places in the world to me.' He gives a big thank you to Mario on the credit sleeve of his debut album, Take Care.

Vocal Coach

In 2010, after being introduced by R&B singer Keri Hilson, Drake decided to join Justin Bieber and Usher in using the services of a vocal coach from Jan Smith Studios. The studios, based in Atlanta, have built up a tremendous reputation in the music industry for excellence and for improving a singer's vocal range.

Smith was due to fly to Canada to start work with Drake, but unfortunately she couldn't make it due to a prior working commitment with Justin Bieber, whom she has been coaching since he was 16. So instead, Smith sent her senior associate Dionne Osborne to work with Drake. Osborne travelled to Toronto to coach Drake early in March 2010, in preparation for his Away From Home tour and various TV and award show commitments. Osborne was actually filmed during a coaching lesson with Drake for the MTV documentary about Drake's life called, *Better Than Good Enough* while travelling on the tour bus.

Smith, who is affectionately known as 'Mama Jan' by her clients, has said of Drake and his team:

> 'It's exciting to have a rap artist and his entire team, who all understand the importance of involving a vocal coach from the beginning of a tour, versus being called in to do the rehab on damaged vocal cords after the fact.'

Wayne Lil

Four-time Grammy Award winner, D'wayne Carter Jr – he dropped the 'D' to distinguish himself from his absent father with the same name – is an American hip-hop recording artist and is best known by his stage name Lil Wayne; other monikers include Wheezy or Lil Tune his grandmother's nickname for him. In 1991 he joined Cash Money Records at the tender age of eleven doing odd jobs around the office, after leaving freestyle raps on the answer machine of the rapper and CEO of the company, Bryan Williams.

Growing up in the tough New Orleans neighbourhood of Hollygrove, he attended Mc Main Secondary School with Cortez Bryant and the pair became firm friends, with Bryant eventually becoming Wayne's manager and later CEO of Young Money Entertainment.

After being paired with Juvenile, BG and Young Turk to form the Hot Boys in 1996 by Cash Money producer Mannie Fresh, they went on to have success with their album Guerilla Warfare in 1999, which reached number one on Billboard's R&B/Hip-Hop album chart. After parting with The Hot Boys to go solo, Wayne released his 1999 debut studio album, The Block Is Hot, which was certified platinum by the RIAA. His sixth album, Tha Carter III became his most successful to date, winning him three Grammy Awards, for Best Rap Album, Best Rap Song, for the single Lollipop and Best Rap Solo Performance, with A Milli. The 2008 album was also certified triple platinum with sales of over 3 million. Wayne went on to found Young Money Entertainment in 2005, as an imprint of Cash Money records.

Early in 2008, Drake was just another rapper trying to make it in the music industry with no record deal and still uploading his mixtapes onto his MySpace page. That was until Jas Prince, the son of Rap-A-Lot founder James Prince, introduced Drake's music to Lil Wayne. After hearing just two songs from the mixtape, Wayne called Drake and had him immediately fly out to join him in Houston. Drake remembers:

> 'He was high out of his mind, getting these big wings tattooed on his body on the tour bus for six hours straight! Then out of nowhere everyone gets on the bus and the bus starts moving. I just kept my mouth shut observing and learning and ended up in Atlanta a week later. It was in Atlanta that we made our first piece of music together.'

He added:

> 'I'll never forget riding on his tour bus, Wayne being asleep and me looking at him thinking to myself that's actually Lil Wayne there and I'm on his bus, just a kid from Toronto.'

The pair developed a close relationship travelling on the tour bus and began to write songs together, which resulted in Stuntin' from Wayne's 2008 Dedication 3 album, Ransom and a remix of Man of the Year, the original finale on Drake's Comeback Season mixtape. The now legendary freestyle Ransom, which featured one verse from each rapper made its debut on the popular hip-hop blog nahright.com on 4 September 2008. Drake credits the Houston trip as the turning point in his music career, and the trip is immortalised in his song November 18th from his So Far Gone mixtape.

After signing his lucrative record deal in 2009, Drake was part of the Young Money Entertainment compilation album, We Are Young Money, on which Wayne performs on every track except Girl I Got You. Fellow Young Money artists Nicki Minaj, Lil Twist, Tyga and Mack Maine also feature on selected tracks off the album.

Drake featured on a total of 5 tracks, including Every Girl and Bedrock, with the latter becoming the most successful single off the album, reaching number one on the Billboard Rap Song chart and number two on the US Billboard Hot 100. In support of the album, Drake joined Lil Wayne and fellow Young Money artists on the Young Money Presents: America's Most Wanted Festival Tour of the US and Canada which started on 29 July 2009.

Wayne is often attributed to giving Drake his nickname Drizzy after shouting out 'Drizzy Drake I love you bwoy!' while performing at the MTV award show in 2008. It was in fact a friend from Toronto called Footz who gave him the nickname, as Drake explains on the track Congratulations, from the So Far Gone mixtape. (see **Drizzy**)

The duo have continued to collaborate together including on the hit single, Right Above It featuring Drake from Wayne's eighth studio album, I Am Not A Human Being, which sold over 2 million copies. The album was released in 2010 while Wayne was still incarcerated in Rikers Island, New York for weapon possession, for which he served 8 months of a 1-year sentence with him recording his verses over the prison telephone. Drake has also co-written and featured on two singles from Wayne's 2011 album Tha Carter IV, with She Will and Its Good. The album sold nearly a million copies in its first week of release and was certified double platinum in 2012.

On 12 March 2013, Wayne was released from hospital after apparently suffering multiple seizures while filming a music video in Los Angeles, before being re-admitted the following day after his staff found him unconscious at home. Drake and Nicki Minaj visited him at the Cedars-Sinai Medical Center before he was finally released, with Wayne putting his health problems down to him having suffered an epileptic seizure. He thanked his fans for their prayers during this time and said he was fine and asked them not to worry.

Wayne went on to release his tenth studio album, I Am Not A Human Being 2, on 26 March 2013 which featured Drake on the track Love Me, and was certified platinum with 1 million sales. The album peaked at number one on the US Billboard Top Rap Album and number two on the R&B/Hip-Hop Album chart.

Wayne has said there will be one more studio album to be called, Tha Carter V before he retires from music and possibly goes into the film industry. In July 2013, Wayne embarked on the second America's Most Wanted Festival tour, a 40-city tour of the US. The tour lasted for 2 months and featured French Montana, Future and T.I. as special guests. Drake joined Lil Wayne on stage during Wheezy's set at Darien Lake PAC, Buffalo, New York to perform his verse from the remix to Migo's Versace. He also embarked on a short European tour in October 2013.

When he is not making music, Wheezy can be found on his skateboard, a sport he took up after he was released from prison.

Weeknd The (Abel Tesfaye)

In 2010 Jeremy Rose, an up-and-coming producer from Toronto, who had already completed the instrumentals and the production for What You Need back in 2007, met Abel Tesfaye while the two were relaxing with mutual friends. Rose started playing a beat, with Tesfaye free-styling over it and they realised they should start making music together.

The duo called themselves 'The Weekend' and went on to record three raw demo songs together: What You Need, a super slow smooth R&B tune, Loft Music, and a version of The Morning, uploading the songs onto their MySpace page.

Around this time the pair teamed up with other musicians, writers and photographers from Toronto to form She's So Lovely, a collective of artists aiming to create video and photography to augment the music. But in December 2010, after a difference of opinion regarding their future music direction, Rose and Tesfaye decided to part company, with Tesfaye deciding to go it alone dropping the 'e' from the band's original name and calling himself, The Weeknd.

Drake first heard about The Weeknd through his manager and creative director, Oliver El-Khatib who played The Weeknd's mixtape, House of Balloons to him. He was immediately knocked out by his great voice on What You Need, The Party and The After Party, with Drake immediately posting the recordings onto his own OVO blog.

Drake said of his young protégé:

> 'Yeah man, this kid has a great voice and I'd love to see what he does. I think the first time I was really sold, I was like super convinced when I heard Crew Love and I was like, man, I need to do this with him for the album, this song is special.'

The Weeknd featured on Drake's album, Take Care as producer and singer on The Ride and Crew Love, and has co-written on four tracks off the album.

- Released: 21 March 2011
- Mixtape: House Of Balloons
- Label: XO
- Length: 49:34
- Producer: Doc Mc Kinney, Illangelo, Jeremy Rose

The Weeknd released House of Balloons in March 2011, as a free nine-track mixtape to critical acclaim onto his own XO label. XO is also the name given to his associates and friends.

He dropped his second mixtape entitled Thursday on 18 August 2011, as a free download through his website, with production by Doc McKinney and Illangelo. Drake featured on the fourth track off the mixtape, The Zone, which he also helped to co-write.

The release of his third mixtape, Echoes of Silence on 21 December 2011, caused his website to crash owing to the substantial number of downloads.

The Weeknd performed his first ever live concert at The Mod Club in Toronto on 24 July 2011, and has gone on to perform at Drake's 2011 and 2012 OVO Festivals at the Molson Amphitheatre, Toronto. In April 2012, he made his first US appearance at the annual Coachella Valley Music and Arts Festival, held in California. Also in September that year he signed to Republic Records in a joint venture with his own XO label and released a compilation album of all his previous hits called Trilogy. Jeremy Rose was acknowledged as producer and writer for three songs off the House of Balloons mixtape.

In 2013, The Weeknd released his debut studio album Kiss Land, with Drake featuring on the third single Live For. He also won two Juno Awards for Breakthrough Artist of The Year and R&B/Soul Recording of The Year for his compilation album Trilogy. In 2014 he will support Drake on his eight-date UK arena tour starting in Manchester on March 11.

West Kanye

Kanye West is an American recording artist, producer and director from Chicago, whom Drake calls one of the most influential people in the music industry alongside Jay Z. Releasing his debut album, The College Dropout in 2004, West has gone on to release five further solo albums and all but one, have reached number one on the US Billboard charts.

His most successful singles include Heartless, from his album 808s & Heartbreak, Stronger from his Graduation album and Gold Digger from Late Registration. All were certified quadruple platinum with over 4 million sales with the RIAA.

In total, West has sold over 12 million albums and 30 million digital downloads, receiving an array of 21 Grammy Awards for various categories and is still very much at the top of his game. Drake has collaborated with West on a number of projects including, when they both featured on Jamie Foxx's single Digital Girl and the hit Forever. West has also co-written and produced Drake's platinum certified single, Find Your Love and he directed the Best I Ever Had basketball-themed music video in 2009.

West appeared at the fourth OVO Festival in 2013 and during his set he informed the crowd that Drake has pushed him and Jay Z to keep raising their game, acknowledging him as the reason for winning the Grammy Award for Best Rap Song with N***as In Paris in 2013.

Drake has said of West:

> 'He shaped a lot of what I do, as far as music goes. We searched the samples to find out where his inspiration comes from because he has one of the best ears in music, period.'

Weston Red Wings

The young Aubrey Graham played hockey for the school team and developed into such a good player, that he was called onto the Weston Red Wings hockey team to play right wing. From there he made it to the Upper Canada College hockey camp, which is generally recognised as providing a good standard of hockey. His mother eventually ended his hockey playing days after he sustained a neck injury from a flailing hockey stick that nearly decapitated him.

What's My Name?

What's My Name? Is the second single from Rihanna's album, Loud and features a rap verse from Drake. The song was certified double platinum by the Recording Industry Association of America, with over 2 million copies sold and reached number one on the US Billboard Hot 100. The duo performed the song together for the first time at the Grammy Award ceremony on 13 February 2011 at the Staples Center, Los Angeles. Drake had three Grammy Nominations on the night for Best Rap Album, Best Rap Performance and Best Rap Performance/Collaboration, failing to win a single award.

- Released: 26 October 2010
- Album: Loud
- Label : Def Jam
- Length: 4:24
- Writers: Mikkel S Eriksen, Tor Erik Hermansen, Ester Dean, Traci Hale, Aubrey Graham.
- Producer: StarGate
- Music Video: Phillip Andelman

The music video, directed by Phillip Andelman was shot in New York over September-October 2010 and was released in November. The action occurs mainly in a store where Drake's road manager CJ Gibson plays the cashier, with Drake performing his verse while he and Rihanna flirt with each other as they buy groceries. The video has had an astronomical 330 million views as of December 2013, and is in the top 30 most viewed videos on YouTube.

White Wine Spritzer

One of Drake's favourite drinks is white wine spritzer and he has suggested that the best way to make the drink is to add together ¾ Santa Margarita Pinot Grigio wine, ¼ club soda and ice, stirring to allow the soda to flow through the wine.

Since he was a teenager, Drake has had a great relationship with Italian restaurants in and around Toronto, especially Sotto Sotto, Sete Messo and Vivoli. This has helped him to amass a great knowledge of wine, partially because he thought this was a way to appear grown up and to impress people. Drake is a wine connoisseur and he has often had to correct a worker in a wine store, about a particular bottle of wine and the vineyard it is from, when he has been mistakenly informed about a wine purchase.

His favourite wines include Italian wines, Gaja Sito Moresco, red Gaia and Tignaello. He has said that he and Justin Timberlake have discussed owning a vineyard in the future and even starting a wine club together. While touring, Pinot Grigio wine is always part of Drake's back stage drinks rider.

William Morris Endeavor

Although the deal was probably sealed months before, Drake's management team officially announced the termination of the contract with International Creative Management talent agency in November 2011. The press release stated that Drake would join William Morris Endeavor (WME) who will represent Drake in all areas worldwide. WME is the largest and oldest global talent agency in the world and is the result of the merger of the William Morris Agency and Endeavor Agency in 2009. The company's stated aim is to create an entertainment-based marketing solution for all clients.

A spokesman for WME stated that the agency's aim for Drake going forward, will be to develop his music, acting (including films) and his philanthropic work. Brent Smith has been named as Drake's future agent.

Williams Bryan and Ronald

Bryan 'Birdman' Williams is an American rapper and record producer and along with his older brother Ronald 'Slim' Williams, founded Cash Money Records in 1991. The duo have executive produced all of Cash Money artists albums and were instrumental in forging the Cash Money/Young Money brand along with Lil Wayne. Cash Money artists also include Lil Wayne, Drake and Nicki Minaj.

Bryan Williams has collaborated on numerous songs with Lil Wayne throughout their careers since Williams' debut album Birdman in 2002. Drake has also featured with Lil Wayne on the singles, Money to Blow and 4 My Town (Play Ball) from Birdman's album, Priceless released in 2009.

Williams and Wayne are due to release their follow-up album to their 2006 hit album, Like Father, Like Son, which reached number one on both the US Billboard Top R&B/Hip-Hop and Billboard Top Rap album charts. The new album due for release in 2013 will be imaginatively called Like Father, Like Son 2.

Williams Pharrell

Pharrell Williams is an American rapper and record producer, known by his stage name Pharrell and is another of Drake's early music idols. He is the lead vocalist and sometime drummer of Drake's favourite early hip-hop/rock band N.E.R.D. Formed in 2001 with Chad Hugo and Shay Haley, N.E.R.D released their first album the gold certified, In Search Of... in 2002.

Drake featured on a remix of the Pharrell produced track, Special off his 2006 mixtape Room for Improvement, which also featured Aion 'Voyce' Clarke – from The Renaissance – on vocals. The same year, Pharrell produced and also featured on the Clipses' second studio album, Hell Hath No Fury, another of Drake's favourite groups.

Since then, Pharrell has built up his reputation in the music industry as a producer, working with numerous big hitters including Kanye West, Jay Z and Madonna and Ludacris.

Pharrell Williams and Hugo formed N.E.R.D as a side project to their main work as part of the successful record production duo The Neptunes. Formed in 1992, the Neptunes have become one of the most successful production companies in music history, producing over twenty Billboard Hot 100 top ten hit singles. Their first number one coming with Britney Spears' I'm A Slave 4 U in 2001 and the duo have gone on to win four Grammy Awards for their production work.

In February 2013, Pharrell won an individual Grammy Award for Best Urban Contemporary album for his production of Frank Ocean's album, Channel Orange. In May 2013, he also featured on the UK number one hit, Get Lucky with French electronic music duo Daft Punk.

Williams Serena

Drake is known as a keen tennis player, so it was perhaps inevitable that when he was invited to partner Serena Williams as her doubles partner, he would jump at the chance. The duo teamed up for the Serena Williams Invitation Event, which is held annually to raise funds for Williams' nominated charity groups. After months of practice games, planned to fit around their busy schedules, the pair hit the court in anticipation and eventually made it through to the final of the event where unfortunately they were defeated.

Later that weekend, Drake was spotted in the crowd cheering Williams at the Rogers Cup Tournament in Toronto, which she went on to win for the second time in her career. In the press there was some suggestion of a romance between the two superstars, but when interviewed about their relationship both have stated that they were just great friends.

Serena Williams is regularly ranked number one in women's singles tennis and is regarded as one of the greatest players of all time. She has also been ranked number one in the women's doubles game with her older sister Venus. Serena has amassed a total of 17 Grand Slam singles titles after winning the US Open final in September 2013.

Williams 'T- Minus' Tyler

Tyler 'T-Minus' Williams, is a Canadian hip-hop and R&B producer from Ajax, Ontario. Interested in music from an early age, Williams started playing drums at Pickering High School, but it was after he had downloaded a digital audio workstation program called Fruity Loops that he started making his own rhymes and songs.

Williams first worked with Drake in 2007 on Drake's second mixtape, Comeback Season, on which he co-produced Replacement Girl with his high school friend Boi-1da. In 2007 Williams signed for Lavish Life Management, founded by his present manager Brendan Malette. Williams acknowledges Malette for giving him the nickname 'T-Minus' and for introducing him to fellow Canadian artist The Weeknd, with whom he has worked closely with since producing his early mixtapes.

After going their separate ways, Drake and Williams met up again in Los Angeles in 2010, with Drake inviting him to work on his Take Care album.

The collaboration resulted in Williams producing four songs off the album, plus The Motto – featuring Lil Wayne – which was one of the bonus tracks on the album. He also had a cameo role in Drake's award-winning video for HYFR, the track he had produced.

Williams has gained a well-deserved reputation for producing smash hits and has gone on to work with numerous other artists including Lil Wayne, Nicki Minaj, DJ Khaled, Rick Ross, Birdman and Mack Maine. He has also produced the single, How Low from Ludacris's gold certified album, Battle of the Sexes. The single was nominated for the Best Rap Solo Performance at the 2011 Grammy Awards, eventually losing out to Eminem's Not Afraid, which was produced by Boi-1da. Williams has also developed a reputation as a song-writer and is credited for both writing and production duties on the triple platinum certified I'm On One, She Will, The Motto, and the platinum certified Moment 4 Life, off Nicki Minaj's Pink Friday album, featuring Drake.

With two Grammy Nominations already under his belt, Williams was finally rewarded for his production work when winning the Broadcast Music, Inc. Top Producer award for 2012.

Wisdom 'Shi' Renee

Toronto R&B artist Renee 'Shi' Wisdom co-wrote the hit single R.I.P. with Drake for Roc Nation's Rita Ora, which topped the UK charts in 2012. Wisdom who hails from a musical family attended York University and is a grade eight graduate of the Royal Conservatory of Music for classical piano. She released her first single Love Speak from her EP, LVSPK in 2011 and continues to make a name for herself both as a performer and a songwriter, with upcoming releases planned including collaboration with Canadian rapper and producer Kardinall Offishall.

Wonder Stevie

Stevie Wonder performed at the 2011 OVO Festival in Toronto, along with Lil Wayne, Rick Ross and The Weeknd. Wonder was initially only supposed to sing two songs, but he ended up performing six songs and completed a 30-minute set. Drake joined the 22-time Grammy winning artist on his hit My Cherie Amour, with the sell-out crowd singing along.

Their first collaboration to hit the airwaves is the track Doing It Wrong, from Drake's Take Care album, with Wonder playing the harmonica outro and also co-produced with '40'. Drake said of the session:

> 'It's an incredible thing I witnessed that night in the studio. He heard a song that he saw some potential in and he added some key pieces that made it come to life.'

Drake has also said of Wonder that he has helped him with his music, told him where to add a couple of things to make it more sonically appealing. The duo are also said to be writing together for a future project.

Wong 'DropxLife' Martin

Martin 'Drop' or 'DropxLife' Wong is a Toronto photographer and graphic designer who is credited for the artwork and design for Drake's Take Care album. Wong is also part of Toronto's famed creative XO crew and works closely with The Weeknd, directing the music videos for Material Girl and The Zone from his Thursday mixtape with both featuring Drake.

Wong is also credited as co-writer and producer on the song Initiation, from The Weeknd's mixtape Echoes of Silence and has used his photographic skills on the cover of the compilation album Trilogy.

Wong is just one of a long line of Toronto professionals whom Drake has helped by using their services in some way. Drake has stated that whenever possible he will give as much help and support to enable fellow Toronto artists and professionals to make an impact in the entertainment industry.

Wong has now entered the vocal side of the music business himself by releasing three mixtapes – Pawncho in 2011, an instrumental mixtape, AllxStar Legends and the nine-track mixtape Furthur, which he released in 2012 – onto his official website for free download. DropxLife tends to drop a track every now and then onto his website and his latest mixtape, Shambhala, with his usual total of nine tracks, was added to the collection in January 2013.

Would You Like A Tour?

On 17 June 2013, Drake announced to press and media outlets that he would be embarking on his Would You Like A Tour? to promote his third studio album, Nothing Was the Same. The 42-city tour of North America with Grammy Award winning R&B singer Miguel and Future as guest artists was due to begin on 25 September in Portland, Oregon and end in Los Angeles on 25 November. But on 20 September a further press release stated that due to 'intense rehearsals and technical production requirements' the now 39-city tour would start on 18 October in Pittsburgh and end on 16 December in Auburn Hills. The 21-date European leg of the tour will commence in Frankfurt, Germany on February 19, 2014.

10-18: Pittsburgh, PA. Target Center
10-19: Philadelphia, PA. Wells Fargo Center
10-21: Montreal, QC. Bell Center
10-22: Ottawa, ON. Scotia Bank Place
10-24: Toronto, ON. Air Canada Center
10-26: Hartford, CT. XL Center
10-27: Newark, NJ. Prudential Center

September continued:
10-28: Brooklyn, NY. Barclays Center
10-30: Boston, MA. TD Garden
10-31: Washington, DC. Verizon Center

November
11-02: Charlotte, NC. Time Warner Cable Arena
11-03: Raleigh, NC. PNC Arena
11-05: Miami, FL. American Airlines Arena
11-06: Tampa, FL. Tampa Bay Times Forum
11-07: Atlanta, GA. Phillips Arena
11-09: New Orleans, LA. New Orleans Arena
11-10: Dallas, TX. American Airlines Center
11-12: San Antonio, TX. AT&T Center
11-13: Houston, TX. Toyota Center
11-16: Pheonix, AZ. US Airlines Center
11-18: Sacramento, CA. Sleep Train Arena
11-19: Oakland, CA. Oracle Arena
11-21: Anaheim, CA. Honda Center
11-22: Las Vegas, NV. MGM Grand Garden Arena
11-24: San Diego, CA. Viejas Center
11-25: Los Angeles, CA. Staples Center
11-28: Vancouver, BC. Rogers Arena Pepsi Live
11-30: Calgary, AB. Scotiabank Saddledome

December
12-01: Edmond, AB. Rexhall Place
12-03: Portland, OR. Rose Garden Arena
12-04: Tacoma, WA. Tacoma Dome
12-07: Kansas City, MO. Sprint Center
12-08: Minneapolis, MN. Target Center
12-09: Indianapolis, IL. Bankers Life Fieldhouse
12-11: St Louis, MO. Scotttrade Center
12-12: Chicago, IL. United Center
12-13: Columbus, OH. Schottenstein Center
12-15: Buffalo, NY. First Niagara Center
12-16: Auburn Hills, MI. The Palace of Auburn Hills

X Director

Julien Lutz, aka Director X is a music video director who has worked across all genres and with some of the biggest names in the music industry. Toronto-born Lutz has worked with Lil Wayne, Nicki Minaj and also Justin Bieber on his smash hit Boyfriend from the album Believe.

Director X directed the music video for Started From the Bottom, the first official single from Drake's third studio album Nothing Was the Same, which was released in 2013. The two had previously collaborated together on the music videos for the 2 Chainz single No Lie, Rick Ross' Diced Pineapples and Drake's Grammy nominated song HYFR.

The music video for HYFR, directed by Director X, was filmed at Miami's Temple Israel and portrays Drake having a Bar Mitzvah, with cameo appearances from Lil Wayne, Trey Songz, Birdman, and Drake's producer Noah Shebib. The video won Best Hip-Hop Video at the 2012 MTV Video Music Awards.

Known as Little X earlier in his career, he directed the music videos for Aaliyah's Come back in One Piece in 2000 and Rihanna's Pon De Replay in 2005, which was filmed in Toronto and features a cameo appearance by Canadian rapper Kardinal Offishall. In 2007 he also directed the music video for Wonder Woman, the first single from Trey Songz debut album Trey Day, which featured a cameo appearance by Drake.

Like many of his contemporaries in the entertainment industry, Director X has diversified into the fashion industry, with his own clothing range called 'X Fit' from the Canadian clothing company Ice Gear Fitness.

In 2013, Director X was nominated at the BET Awards for Best Video Direction and won the MuchMusic Director of The Year for Started From the Bottom.

Director X's Music Videos featuring Drake

Year	Artist	Single	Featuring
2007	Trey Songz	Wonder Woman	Drake
2012	Rick Ross	Diced Pineapples	Drake, Wale
2012	2 Chainz	No Lie	Drake
2012	Shanell	So Good/6AM	Drake, Lil Wayne
2012	Drake	HYFR	
2013	Drake	Started From the Bottom	
2013	Drake	Worst Behavior	

XX Jamie

Jamie Smith is an English producer, mix artist and rapper better known by his stage name, Jamie XX. Well known throughout the music industry as being one of the three members of the band The XX, Smith is also noted for his work as a solo artist and music producer. The XX have also been successful in winning the highly prestigious UK Mercury Prize in 2010 for their debut album XX.

The award is chosen by music industry executives and journalists, with the winners receiving a £2,000 prize and often gaining an increase in album sales and popularity.

The band was nominated for Best British Group at the 2013 BRIT Awards.

The duo met while Drake was touring the UK as part of his 2010 Away From Home tour, with Smith going on to produce the title song off Drake's second studio album Take Care, featuring Rihanna, which samples Smith's remix of I'll Take Care of You. Drake had said that he wanted to work with the Londoner again on his upcoming third studio album Never Was the Same saying 'I really want him to have a big presence on this album, so we can take it a step further.' Unfortunately due to work commitments it never happened.

XO

The XO team is a Toronto-based creative group consisting of many talents: singing from The Weeknd; rapper Omari Shakir; photography/filming through Hyghly Alleyne and Lamar Taylor; production skills by Martin Wong; and management covered by Jake Wilson.

Formed in 2007, the group is now very much associated with Drake's own Toronto-based OVO crew. The two teams often work together on projects – with The Weeknd featuring on Crew Love, Martin Wong responsible for the artwork and design on Drake's Take Care album, and Alleyne and Taylor directing three videos for Drake – winning numerous awards.

Whenever Drake's October's Very Own (OVO) crew and The Weeknd's (XO) crew collaborate, the moniker OVOXO is always used. Drake has worn an OVOXO t-shirt while performing at his OVO Festival in Toronto.

XO's motto is 'till we overdose.'

Y

YOLO

YOLO, the acronym for You Only Live Once, has been used since the early 2000s after allegedly being uttered first by Adam Mesh on the third season of NBC's reality show *Average Joe*. Many people have gone on to have the phrase tattooed on various parts of their bodies as an inspirational statement to live life to the full. Drake has made the words famous owing to his song, The Motto.

Rapper Rick Ross has also mentioned the phrase on his Rich Forever song, which featured John Legend from his 2012 album, God Forgives I Don't. Drake and Ross were planning to release an album called YOLO, which was provisionally due to be dropped in 2012, but the project had to be postponed due to Ross having a health scare in October 2011, with the pair still committed to the project. Drake has also mentioned YOLO on the Take Care album credit sleeve on his tribute to Ross.

The phrase has also appeared in Drake's episode of the spoof TV show *Punk'd*. When the secret service agent who was travelling with Drake turned round to him during the ride to allegedly meet the Vice President of America, and after talking about how much he admired him and enjoyed his music, said YOLO with Drake smiling in acknowledgement.

Young Artist Award

The Young Artist Award recognises young people for their work in the entertainment industry. Established in 1978 as the Youth in Film award, its name was changed in 1987 and the award ceremony is held in California each year.

Drake has won the award once, from five nominations, when in 2002 he was part of the *Degrass: The Next Generation* cast who won Best Ensemble in a TV series or Drama Award.

Young Artists for Haiti

After the 7.1 magnitude earthquake hit Haiti on 12 January 2010, entertainment bosses Bob Ezrin, Randy Lennox and David Sleight, mobilised Canadian musicians in an effort to raise funds for the people affected. In less than a week over 50 musicians had gathered to raise funds for the charity. The collective, known as Young Artists for Haiti gathered at Bryan Adams's Warehouse Studios in Vancouver, BC to record Wavin' Flag. The song, originally recorded by the K'naans, was reworked to include lyrics specific to the stricken country, with Drake performing a solo verse near the end of the song.

The record, which featured other notable Canadians including Justin Bieber, Avril Lavigne, Kardinal Offishall, Nelly Furtado and Michael Buble, reached number one on the Canadian Hot 100 chart and won a Juno Award for Single of the Year in 2011.

Young Money Entertainment

Young Money Entertainment is an American record label and brand founded by Lil Wayne in 2005. The American label is an imprint of Wayne's Cash Money record label and is distributed by Republic Records in the US and Universal worldwide. The Rappers Curren$y and Boo were the first artists to sign with the Young Money Entertainment label.

Since the release of their first mixtape in 2005, Young Money: The Mixtape Volume 1, which featured Mack Maine, Curren$y, Boo and Wayne, the label has gone on to release eight number one albums, including three by Wayne, three by Drake with Thank Me Later, Take Care and Nothing Was the Same and Nicki Minaj's Pink Friday.

- Released: 21 December 2009
- Album: We Are Young Money
- Label: Young Money Entertainment, Cash Money Records
- Length: 65:12
- Singles: Every Girl, Bedrock, Roger That
- Producers: Kane Beatz, Tha Bizness, Chase N Cashe, Infamous, Cool & Dre, B Carr, David Banner, Willy Will, DL Mecca, Mr Pryo

Soon after signing Nicki Minaj and Drake, Young Money Entertainment released a compilation album, We Are Young Money in 2009. The album sold over 140,000 in its first week of release and went on to be certified gold by the RIAA with sales of over 500,000. The album reached number one on the US Billboard Rap album chart, with Drake featuring on the first two singles, Every Girl and the most successful single from the album Bedrock.

Drake was the first artist from Young Money, excluding Wayne himself, to reach the number one position with his debut studio album, Thank Me Later.

The current roster of Young Money Entertainment artists includes, Drake, Lil Wayne, Nicki Minaj, Tyga and Mack Maine. The presidency of the company has changed over the years between Wayne, Cortez Bryant and more recently, the current President of the label Mack Maine. Future Young Money Entertainment releases scheduled for 2014 include: Nicki Minaj's third studio album Pink Friday: The Pink Print.

Young Money Entertainment released the first compilation album by Young Money and Cash Money stars called Rich Gang on 23 July 2013. The album contained contributions from Nicki Minaj, Birdman, French Montana, Tyga and Wayne with the first single, Tapout released in March 2013.

Young People's Theatre

When Aubrey Graham was around five years old, his mother, who had secured him an agent – Aubrey featured in print catalogues and commercials – also enrolled him with the Young People's Theatre, based in Toronto. Her aim was to try to keep him interested in as many activities as possible. He attended every Saturday and the young Aubrey had his first public singing part during the theatre's production of *Les Miserables*. He remembers being taken aback when people actually clapped the performance because they had liked it and not because it had finished.

Founded in 1966 by Susan Douglas Rubes, the theatre is the largest for young audiences in Canada and is based at 165 Front Street East, Toronto.

Z

Zombie Mike

Michael Coleman is an American rapper and producer from Willingboro, New York better known as Mike Zombie. Zombie produced Started From the Bottom, the first single from Drake's third studio album, Nothing Was the Same. Zombie has also added his own freestyle to the song and has uploaded the version onto iTunes. The original song premiered on Drake's October's Very Own blog on 1 February 2013 and was the BET Hip-Hop Track of the Year.

Drake was introduced to Zombie by Queen's rapper Hollow Da Don, both of whom are with the Loyalty Over Money crew. Hollow Da Don is a renowned rap battler and a BET 106 Parks Freestyle Friday Champion, who won the rap battle for seven consecutive weeks in 2006. Drake is a huge fan of the rap battle scene, which features rappers, Iron Solomon, The Saurus and Hollow Da Don. In August 2011 he had a $25,000 bet with Nelly on the Hollow Da Don Versus Hitman Holla battle, when they went head to head over Drake's Headlines beat. Drake won his bet when Hollow was again victorious.

Mike Zombie is signed to Drake's OVO record label.

PHOTOGRAPHIC ACKNOWLEDGEMENTS

The author and publishers would like to thank the following copyright holders for their kind permission to reproduce the pictures in this book.

Front Cover: Matt Barnes; Dr Billy Ingham/Getty Images; Jeffery Mayer/Getty Images;

Johnny Nunez/Getty Images; Kevin Mazur/Getty Images;

Kevin Winter/Getty Images; Larry Buacca/Getty Images;

Kevork Djansezian/Getty Images; Michael Buckner/Getty Images;

Gary Miller/Getty Images; Aby Baker/Getty Images;

George Pimentel/Getty Images; Back Cover: City of Toronto.

Every reasonable effort has been made to acknowledge correctly and trace copyright holders of material and photographs in this book. The publisher and author apologise for any unintended errors or omissions, and will be pleased to insert the appropriate acknowledgement in any subsequent future edition(s) brought to their attention.

Chronology

1986
24 October: Aubrey Graham born in Toronto.

1999
Aubrey Graham has his Bar mitzvah party in Toronto.

2001
4 November: Graham makes his first appearance in *Degrassi: The Next Generation* in an episode entitled *Family Politics* as James 'Jimmy' Brooks.

2002
7 April: With fellow cast members, Aubrey Graham wins best ensemble in a TV Series/Comedy or Drama for *Degrassi: The Next Generation*.

2004
10 December: Graham's character 'Jimmy Brooks' is shot on *Degrassi: The Next Generation* and is confined to a wheelchair.

2005
10 June: As one of the most popular cast members, Graham takes part in a series of mini documentaries entitled *Degrassi Unscripted*.

2006
14 February: Release of Drake's first mixtape, Room for Improvement.

2007
February: Drake appears in his first music video on Jenna G's single Change You.

March:
Drake's official fan site allthings-fresh.net goes live.

30 April: Replacement Girl video features on BET.

October: Release of Drake's second mixtape, Comeback season.

2008
August: Lil Wayne is given a mixtape of Drake's music by Jas Prince. Drake travels to Houston to meet Wayne.

30 November: Aubrey Graham's last appearance on *Degrassi; The Next Generation.* The eighth episode of the eighth season Lost In Love: Pt1 is shown on CTV.

2009
13 February: Release of Drake's third mixtape So Far Gone.

29 June: Drake's management team, Hip Hop since 1978 and Cortez Bryant from Bryant Management, negotiated a lucrative recording deal with Young Money /Cash Money Aspire/Universal Records.

31 July: Drake reinjures his knee whilst performing at Camden, NY on the Lil Wayne America's Most Wanted tour.

15 September: Release of the So Far Gone EP.

2010
2 March: Appears with Jay Z at Madison Square Garden, New York.

9 March: Over, the first single from the Thank Me Later album released

5 April: Away From Home tour starts at Slippery Rock University.

15 June: Release of Drake's first studio album, Thank Me Later.

2 August: First OVO Music Festival held in Toronto. Jay Z and Eminem make guest appearances.

20 September: Start of Light Dreams & Nightmares tour in Miami.

6 November: Light Dreams & Nightmares tour ends in Las Vegas.

2011
31 July: Second OVO Festival held in Toronto features Stevie Wonder.

12 November: Release of second studio album Take Care.

4 November: Drake's grandmother Evelyn Sher passed away on Thanksgiving Day.

2012
31 Jan: Take Care certified platinum by the RIAA with sales of over 1 million copies.

5 August: Third OVO Music Festival held in Toronto featured Rick Ross and Nicki Minaj.

2013
6 February: Started From the Bottom, the first single from Nothing Was the Same released.

10 February: Drake wins his first Grammy Award for Best Rap Album with Take Care.

17 June: Drake announces his Would You Like A Tour? 41 City, North American Tour will start on 25 September.

5 August: Fourth OVO Festival featured Kanye West and Lil Wayne.

24 September: Drake's third studio album, Nothing Was the Same released.

October: Hold On We're Going Home, released on 7 August is certified platinum with over 1 million sales.

18 October: Start of the re-scheduled Would You Like A Tour? in Pittsburgh.